Singing Penguins & Puffed-Up Toads

William L. Coleman

 Bethany Fellowship INC.
MINNEAPOLIS, MINNESOTA 55438

Published by Bethany Fellowship, Inc.
6820 Auto Club Road, Minneapolis, Minnesota 55438
Printed in the United States of America

Library of Congress Cataloging in Publication Data

Coleman, William L.
    Singing penguins and puffed-up toads.

    Summary: Presents thoughts for meditation concerning the wonders of the world's oceans.
        1. Children—Prayer-books and devotions—English. [1. Prayer books and devotions. 2. Ocean] I. Title.
BV4870.C635   242'.62   81-1079
ISBN 0-87123-554-4   AACR2

Biographical Sketch

WILLIAM L. COLEMAN is a graduate of the Washington Bible College in Washington, D.C., and Grace Theological Seminary in Winona Lake, Indiana.

He has pastored three churches: a Baptist church in Michigan, a Mennonite church in Kansas, and an Evangelical Free Church in Aurora, Nebraska. He is a Staley Foundation lecturer.

The author of 75 magazine articles, his by-line has appeared in *Christianity Today, Eternity, Good News Broadcaster, Campus Life, Moody Monthly, Evangelical Beacon,* and *The Christian Reader.* Besides the children's devotional series, Coleman is also the author of the new Chesapeake Charlie series, mysteries for ages 10-14.

Other Books by the Same Author

Devotionals for families with young children

Counting Stars, meditations on God's creation.

My Magnificent Machine, devotionals centered around the marvels of the human body.

Listen to the Animals, lessons from the animal world.

On Your Mark, challenges from the lives of well-known athletes.

More About My Magnificent Machine, more devotionals describing parts of the human body and how they reflect the genius of the Creator.

Singing Penguins and Puffed-Up Toads, devotionals about the creatures of the sea.

Devotionals for very small children

The Good Night Book, bedtime inspirationals (especially for those who may be afraid of the dark).

Today I Feel Like a Warm Fuzzy, devotionals for small children which help them to identify and learn how to respond to their own feelings and emotions.

The Chesapeake Charlie Series

Mysteries for ages 10-14

Chesapeake Charlie and the Bay Bank Robbers

Chesapeake Charlie and Blackbeard's Treasure

Contents

A World of Adventure

Get ready to dive thousands of feet into the ocean. In this watery world you can see the large eyes of a leggy octopus. You will catch a gleam from the sharp white teeth of the shark. Before long, though, you will be greeted by the friendly grin of a dolphin.

Today people are diving deeply into the sea. Tomorrow people could be actually living there in bubble cities!

As you read, you will get a small taste of this adventurous world under the water. You can also learn more about what the heavenly Father and His Son have done for us.

William L. Coleman
Aurora, Nebraska

one

The Friendly Dolphin

Would you like to meet a dolphin? Not just to see one or pat it on the head, but to actually be its friend? Perhaps you could join it every morning for a swim or even do a ballet with one!

Some people have actually done these things and more with wild dolphins. They are not fish, you know. No one knows for sure how smart these mammals are, but a few scientists believe that dolphins are extremely intelligent.

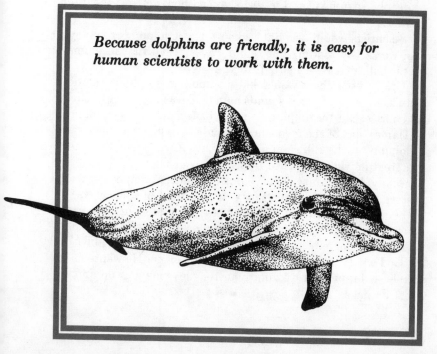

Because dolphins are friendly, it is easy for human scientists to work with them.

For example, after scuba diving for many years, one lady suddenly discovered that she had a new friend. Each day when she went for a swim a dolphin began to swim alongside her. The lady would swim in patterns and the dolphin would copy each motion. Even graceful, ballet-like turns were copied step by step. One day, however, after six months of close companionship, the dolphin disappeared, never to be seen again.

Where had the dolphin come from? And why did it leave? Dolphins usually travel in groups called "schools" and are seldom alone. But every so often, over the years, dolphins have left the "school" and become friendly with people.

One man who believed that dolphins enjoy people invented an underwater instrument similar to an accordion. He took this black box under the sea and played it to the dolphins. The dolphins seemed more than happy with this "music." Three or four of them began to soar through the water to the tune of the song as if they had been trained to do so.

If you want to personally meet some wild but friendly dolphins, travel to Shark Bay, Australia. There a school of dolphins often visits the beach. These dolphins are calm and allow many children to pet them.

Because dolpins are friendly, it is easy for human scientists to work with them. Scientists want to know how a dolphin can dive so deeply, so quickly and return again without getting sick. Man cannot.

Scientists would also like to know how a dolphin's sonar system works. By sending out sound waves they can find a small metal ball at least a football field away.

Other researchers would like to know more about the dolphin's language. To us it sounds merely like a long string of clicks and noises. But the dolphin seems to have a definite vocabulary.

James, one of the men who was close to Jesus, may have seen a dolphin. In the Bible James wrote that it was easier to tame a sea creature than for us to tame our own tongues.

Many of us know what James meant. A dolphin can be trained to do amazing things for a fish dinner. But when we try to train our own tongue, it still seems to get totally out of control. We say some really dumb things at times. Later we wish we had kept quiet. Some of the things we say hurt people terribly.

God wants us to let Him control our tongue. He wants us to ask Jesus for help. If we don't, our tongues may go wild and do great damage.

"Men have trained, or can train, every kind of animal or bird that lives and every kind of reptile and fish, but no human being can tame the tongue" (James 3:7, 8, TLB).

1. What do scientists want to know about dolphins?
2. Which country has a special beach where dolphins allow children to pet them?
3. Have you ever said something that you wish you hadn't? What *should* you have said then?

Help us use our tongues to say good things, Lord.

two

A Good Father

Nature is filled with many excellent mothers and fathers as well as a few who are not so great. But it would be hard to find a more caring dad than the American Sea Catfish. He is not only helpful but also very patient.

As soon as mother catfish lays the eggs, father catfish takes over. Each egg is laid one at a time and is about one inch around. Father catfish opens his large mouth and carefully tucks each egg inside it. There are at least 10 eggs, but some catfish have been found with as many as 55 eggs packed inside their jowls.

Carrying eggs in his mouth is no small sacrifice for the father catfish. It may take a month before these eggs hatch. During this time Dad will not eat one bite of food for himself.

The American Sea Catfish is called a mouth-breeding fish. Most eggs in the sea never hatch. For instance, an octopus lays thousands of eggs which are merely eaten by other creatures. Father catfish, however, makes sure his eggs live. Each egg actually hatches inside Dad's mouth. If we could see inside, we might notice a couple of dozen eggs plus a few hatched fish swimming around. We can only hope that the father never hiccups and swallows his own baby fish.

Father catfish's mouth works like an incubator. It keeps the eggs protected at just the right temperature until the new fish are ready to hatch. The sea catfish makes a fantastic father.

We would like to have a fantastic father also. Both our mother and father are very important to us, and we want to be able to live with both of them. But sometimes life doesn't go the way we want it to. Once in a while a parent dies while the children are still young. Some parents even get divorced and move away from each other.

Whatever happens in our family, one person never changes. We have a Father in heaven who is the same today, tomorrow, and forever.

The catfish father does some great things, but naturally he isn't perfect. All fathers make mistakes, even the best of them—that is, all fathers except the God who watches over us. We can talk to Him twenty-four hours a day. He even knows how many hairs we have!

"See how very much our heavenly Father loves us, for he allows us to be called his children—think of it—and we really are!" (1 John 3:1, TLB).

1. How many eggs can some catfish carry?
2. How long before a catfish egg might hatch?
3. In what ways is God a Father to us?

Thanks for caring, heavenly Father.

three

Farming the Sea

Can you imagine a tractor or a combine working on the ocean floor? This is no longer a dream of science fiction. These and other underwater machines are already at work planting and harvesting sea crops.

Sea farming is a little different from farming in Nebraska. The underwater farmer wears an oxygen tank and a helmet. However, he does ride a tractor and he does help feed the world.

This kind of farming has many purposes. In the Pacific Ocean there are pearl and oyster farmers. They keep a crop of oysters attached to poles to grow pearls. A tiny piece of shell is inserted in each oyster and they hope it will develop into a pearl.

Much of the seaweed we see floating on the water is actually kelp. This weed is plentiful in the ocean and grows a foot or two a day. Farmers are busy harvesting the crop for industrial use and energy. Many people in Japan eat kelp.

If you don't want to farm in the ocean, maybe you would rather be a fish rancher. Fish ranchers are already in business on the shores of China, Japan, and the Philippines. Instead of taking their chances on catching fish the normal way, they mark off an area and grow their own.

One of the problems with fish ranching is how to fence off your livestock. A net fence seems like a good idea, but it always needs repair. Some ranchers have installed pipes which give off bubbles. When these bubbles rise in a steady stream, the fish will not swim through them.

Instead of being a wheat or corn farmer, you might choose to produce fish flour. It's already being done. Fish flour is made by turning dried fish into powder. It's inexpensive, and it leaves no fish taste. Half the fish now caught are either thrown back or destroyed. Since any fish can be used to make this flour, the savings are tremendous.

Fish flour is a big help in areas where farm land is small or the ground is too hard. Fish is high in protein and can help millions of starving people.

Presently, we receive only one percent of our food from the sea. With improved farming, the produce from this source could be greatly increased.

The next chocolate pudding you eat may be made from fish flour and seaweed. Someday the jelly you spread on your bread may come from an ocean farm.

Jesus Christ taught that it is important to feed the hungry. When we help feed the starving, it is just as if we were giving food to Christ himself. Maybe farming the sea is one more way God wants us to use His world wisely.

"For I was hungry and you fed me; I was thirsty and you gave me water; I was a stranger and you invited me into your homes" (Matt. 25:35, TLB).

1. Name two sea products that are being farmed.
2. How much of our food comes from the sea?
3. How do Christians help feed the hungry? What is something your family could do?

Our world can produce enough food for everyone. Show us, Lord, how to use all of it as you have planned.

four

The Jellyfish Sting

If you ever get a chance to swim in the ocean, look out for umbrella-shaped blobs of jelly before you jump in. I don't mean the kind of jelly you put on your toast in the morning! Instead, I mean a jellyfish—the kind that my children found when they went swimming in Chesapeake Bay.

The jellyfish is a slimy looking creature with long stringy legs called tentacles. Its head is shaped like a mushroom or an umbrella. And the body is so clear that you almost can see through it.

Jellyfish give a painful sting if they brush against you. However, careful swimmers can pick them up by the head and carry them out of the water.

If people are careful to watch where they are going, most jellyfish can be avoided. These sea creatures are not fast movers. Often their speed is controlled by the tide and waves. Jellyfish can swim a little by pumping their bodies, but they could never catch a person.

Usually they merely hang in the water and wait for a tiny fish or microscopic animal to pass by. Then they sting. This sting paralyzes the fish or tiny animal and makes it easier for the jellyfish to eat his prey. A jellyfish doesn't sting everything, however. The pompano fish can make its home under a jellyfish without ever being stung.

After spending three days at Chesapeake Bay, our son came in from swimming with large red marks on his left arm. He had been stung by a jellyfish, but it hurt less than the sting of a bee.

When something touches a stinger, tiny needles dart out and stick through the flesh.

His mother put something on it and he was soon back in the water.

Jellyfish legs or tentacles are covered with stingers. When something touches a stinger, tiny needles dart out and stick through the flesh. These needles shoot poison which can paralyze or kill a fish but merely sting a human being.

There are some relatives of the jellyfish which can be extremely dangerous to humans. The Portuguese man-of-war is larger and contains more poison. Its sting can make a person very sick.

Sometimes the water is so crowded with jellyfish that it is unsafe for swimming because the swimmers would be stung so often they would become miserable. One sailor sighted a group of jellyfish spread out over 250 miles. He estimated there were over one million jellyfish in this one area.

The jellyfish often gets into trouble because it can't swim better. If a big wave pushes it into a human, it is often killed. If a large fish decides to eat it, there is no way for the jellyfish to get away. Jellyfish are merely tossed about in the water.

The same thing can happen to us if we don't have faith in Jesus Christ. One day we might do what is right, but the next day we may do something rotten. One minute we want God to lead us. The next minute we don't care what God says. This type of person is very unstable. Everytime a new wave comes, he is pushed along with it wherever it goes. Faith in Jesus Christ, however, holds us steady.

"But let him ask in faith, nothing wavering. For he that wavereth is like a wave of the sea, driven with the wind and tossed" *(James 1:6, KJV).*

1. How do jellyfish catch food?
2. How does a jellyfish get around?
3. How can a person change from being like a jellyfish?

Thank you, Jesus Christ, for giving us stability in our lives.

five

Don't Drink the Water

Few people are as far from drinking water as the man in a lifeboat on the ocean. As one poet has said, "Water, water everywhere, but not a drop to drink."

What would happen if this lone human started drinking the salty sea water? He would soon find his thirst growing greater rather than less. If he continued to drink, he would become terribly sick. He might even become delirious. After a while his kidneys would cease to work. Finally he would die.

Man is unable to drink sea water because it contains approximately 3.5 percent salt. While this may sound like only a small amount, it is enough to be very dangerous.

The sea is a fascinating collection of minerals which we can't see. In one cubic mile of ocean water there are over 2 tons of nickel, 235 tons of iodine, and 38 pounds of gold. Before we start mining the sea water, however, one thing should be remembered. We would have to "mine" one million gallons before we removed one penny's worth of gold.

How did all these minerals become a part of the sea water? For instance, water doesn't come out of the sky with salt in it. In fact, when man catches rainwater, he has a fairly pure liquid although it may pick up some substance from the polluted air.

After it reaches earth, water picks up minerals from several sources. It runs down mountains, curves through riverbeds, and washes across plains. During its journey to the sea, it collects many samples of different minerals. Then, when it has run its course to the sea, the minerals have few places to go so they settle to the ocean floor.

Already waiting for it are large salt deposits. They are resting on the floor where they have flavored the sea for years. The Gulf of Mexico has a huge salt dome stretching its shoulders for five miles.

Researchers are spending large amounts of money in order to discover how to take salt out of the water. If they are successful, irrigation will be possible in many areas of the world which are now dry.

In some ways people are like ocean water. We need to have our lives changed. Selfishness, anger, and every type of sin are as dangerous to us as drinking salt water. God wants to take these things out of us and put His goodness into us. This change can happen to anyone. People have given their lives to Jesus Christ and have asked Him to change them. Only He can do this.

We are beginning to change salty water to fresh, but God has been making selfish people into kind people for a long time.

"Can you pick olives from a fig tree, or figs from a grapevine? No, and you can't draw fresh water from a salty pool.

"If you are wise, live a life of steady goodness, so that only good deeds will pour forth" (James 3:12, 13, TLB).

1. Name some minerals that are in the ocean.
2. What would happen if you drank very much ocean water?
3. Do you know someone who has become a Christian? How was this person changed?

We thank you, God, for new life in Christ.

six

The Toughest Glue

What are those little shells you see on the bottom of boats or clinging to the posts at piers? If you grab hold of them while swimming, you can get a nasty scratch on your hands. These tough little shells are called barnacles.

They're more than just a nuisance. When they glue themselves to the bottoms of boats, the small shells can become a real problem. They slow down the boats by dragging in the water. Barnacles can also cause rust on some vessels. When my son and I went sailing in the Puget Sound, we saw signs which advertised the services of scuba divers; for a few dollars they would scrape the barnacles off the bottom of your boat.

Not only do barnacles attach themselves to hard surfaces, but they also glue their shells to marine life. Some starfish have tiny "scissors" that they use to clip off barnacles.

Barnacles are living creatures. When they are first born, barnacles are so small they barely can be seen. There are two types of barnacles: the Gooseneck and the Acorn variety. These little creatures are often eaten by larger sea animals. Those who escape being eaten usually float around for a while until they find a place to settle. This is done by pasting their backs onto a surface with a special glue they secrete. Once its tough glue hardens, the barnacle is terribly hard to remove.

As it sits there, attached to a boat bottom, the barnacle gets ready to eat. Barnacles can do this neatly by opening their secret doors. These shells slide open like elevator doors. Part of the barnacle hurriedly reaches out and grabs small pieces of food. When the doors are closed it looks like no one lives there.

Barnacles cannot eat unless they are under water. However, they also make good eating. Fish, birds, and snails often have lunch at a barnacle restaurant. This is why we see so many empty barnacle shells around sea water.

Scientists are interested in barnacles for several reasons. First, they would like to learn a way to keep them from sticking on boats. Second, scientists want to know how this glue is made. If we could do the same thing, we might be able to glue wood, iron, and even human bones as never before.

As with all of nature, even this glue can't last forever. It is possible for barnacles to be worn off or scraped away. The only things that last forever are in Jesus Christ. For instance, Jesus Christ is our friend and our Savior and He will never go away.

Even in the times when we are at our worst, Christ sticks close. His love for us is tougher than any glue in the world.

"For God has said, 'I will never, never fail you nor forsake you' " (Heb. 13:5, TLB).

1. What is a barnacle?
2. How does a barnacle eat?
3. How long will Jesus love you? How long should we love Him?

Thanks, Lord Jesus, for sticking close when the waves get rough.

seven

Waves Gone Wild

How high is your house? Scientists have measured ocean waves at 60 feet high. That would be higher than almost any of our homes.

Some sailors insist that waves can be even larger. In 1933 the Navy tanker *Ramapo* was sitting fairly level when a monstrous wave crashed across it. The crew claims it hit the vessel at 112 feet high.

The next time you hear about someone crossing the ocean in a small boat, remember these waves sizes. It is a tremendously dangerous voyage in a tiny craft.

Not only are waves big, but they are powerful. One series of waves began to attack a British shore and did not quit until it had destroyed a 2,600-ton concrete wall.

During a particularly rough night at Tillamook Rock, the restless sea revealed its enormous power. The waves picked up a 135-pound rock and smashed it against the lighthouse 100 feet above sea level.

Waves at the beach are fun to use for surfing or just to play in. They are also fascinating to watch. However, we should always respect their strength.

Often the violent waves begin some place far away and build up as they cross the ocean. In 1955 there was an earthquake in Lisbon, Portugal. The force of the quake sent waves rolling until they eventually flooded the West Indies, thousands of miles away.

Other floods are caused by earthquakes beneath the sea.

These quakes cause a great upheaval which brings terrible disaster.

A single wave does not travel across the entire ocean. Instead, one wave pushes another wave which in turn pushes another, and so on.

Waves are so important to safe travel that they are studied; wave predictions are given just like weather reports. The Navy Oceanographic Office issues wave forecasts twice a day.

People study wave movement in hopes of using waves for energy. As they steadily beat against the shores, scientists are inventing ways to use their power to produce electricity.

A wave does not have to be only in the ocean to be powerful. Gigantic waves on lakes can tear large ships apart.

Fishermen during the life of Christ knew how dangerous waves could be. A sudden squall could hit Galilee and sink a boat in a few minutes.

Jesus was asleep on a boat when one of these squalls came. The experienced fishermen were immediately afraid. When Jesus woke up He merely told the waves to calm down. The waves instantly obeyed.

If God tells nature to do something, nature will always do it. He wants people to be like the waves and obey Him.

"So he spoke to the storm: 'Quiet down,' he said, and the wind and waves subsided and all was calm!" (Luke 8:24, TLB).

1. How high can waves become?
2. How can waves be used?
3. Why is it important to God that He be obeyed?

Most of the time we know what is right, Lord. Help us to do it!

eight

A Walrus Shopping Center

Are you looking for a household pet? Don't get a walrus!

The biggest problem with keeping a walrus is the fact that it weighs up to two tons. To stay alive, this large sea animal has to eat 100 pounds of food daily. His favorite food is shellfish. He gobbles down thousands of clams every day. The shells are spit out and the meat is quickly swallowed.

If the walrus' size and food bill do not bother you, think about his tusks. He has two large teeth which point straight down. The walrus uses them as dangerous weapons. If a walrus wants a particular place to sleep or a particular meal, he may be willing to fight for it.

Before you buy a walrus pet, you will also need to install a large swimming area. They can dive 300 feet and stay under for 20 to 30 minutes. Walruses are clumsy on land, but they are excellent swimmers.

Walruses don't like to live alone; actually, they like to live in groups of two or three hundred!

There is no need to worry about clothing. A walrus can live in hot or cold weather. He has three inches of blubber or fat to protect him from the temperature. The walrus also has an amazing blood system. Blood can move quickly around his body to offset heat or cold. After diving, a walrus may be a reddish brown because his blood has moved to the surface of his skin to adjust to the temperature change.

Eskimos do not keep walruses as pets, but they do hunt them for practically all of their needs. Catching a walrus is like going

He has three inches of blubber or fat to protect him from the temperature.

to your local shopping center. Walrus meat is used to feed both people and dogs. Walrus muscles are made into ropes. Their ivory tusks are turned into spoons or art carvings. The Eskimo uses every part of the walrus. Even its whiskers are kept for toothpicks.

Living in the frozen northland is difficult. People need to put everything to good use in order to survive. Fortunately God has given the walrus to the Eskimo to meet most of his needs.

All of us have needs too. They go much deeper than food and clothing, though. We need to have our sins forgiven. We need to know what God is like. And we need to know that God loves us. These are real needs. And only God knows how to satisfy these needs. That is why He sent Jesus Christ to live and die for us.

"And it is he who will supply all your needs from his riches in

glory, because of what Christ Jesus has done for us" (Phil. 4:19, TLB).

1. What does a walrus eat?
2. How do Eskimos use walruses?
3. What needs does Jesus Christ meet?

You, Lord Jesus, have given us what we could not give ourselves.

nine

What Is a Sea Horse?

When you go swimming, the last thing you expect to see is a horse. You probably never will, but don't be surprised if you see a fish that looks like one. Its tiny head is shaped like a horse and it swims sitting up straight as if galloping some place.

Sea horses can be found in many parts of the world. They are most often seen in warm water.

Most fathers in nature have little to do with their babies. A few will, but it is rare when the father cares at all. With the father sea horse, though, it is another story.

The mother lays her eggs into a pouch located on the father's stomach. Then, just like a kangaroo, father sea horse carries the 200 eggs around in his pouch until a month and a half later when they begin to hatch and pop out.

Most sea horses are small. Even when full grown they stretch only to half a foot. Some never become bigger than a couple of inches. If you want to see the big ones, visit the West Coast. There they reach a complete foot in length.

Sea horses enjoy eating. They have no teeth—only a tube-shaped nose. If it is hungry, a sea horse often sits down on a weed and waits for food. It hooks its little tail onto the branch and holds on. Tiny bits of animal and plant life called plankton drift by and the sea horse sucks it in. Some plankton are so small you can't see them without a microscope.

Most of us have seen small sea horses in stores or advertised in the paper. They make cute aquarium pets but often don't last long. It is very hard to create the exact water and food conditions they need.

Sea horses enjoy eating. They have no teeth— only a tube-shaped nose.

Whatever type of creature we are, sometimes we forget the many things our fathers do for us. God gave us something special when He gave us a dad. Like a sea horse he plays a terrific part in helping our lives. Why don't you give him a thank you or a hug today?

"Honor your father and mother. This is the first of God's Ten Commandments that ends with a promise" (Eph. 6:2, TLB).

1. Where is a sea horse's pouch?
2. How many eggs does a sea horse carry?
3. List some good things your father has done for you.

Thank God for fathers.

ten

Surprising Icebergs

The sea is full of sudden changes and surprises. One minute its waters may be calm but then in a short time it's possible for a raging storm to appear. When everything is motionless again, maybe half a dozen porpoises will come skipping across the surface.

One of the biggest surprises of the sea, however, is the floating iceberg. If we see an iceberg we may be fooled by its appearance. There is far more ice under the water than there is on top. Possibly 90 percent of the ice is hidden beneath the surface.

Icebergs are beautiful and interesting, but they are also extremely dangerous. Many people have lost their lives because they were not careful to keep their boats away from them.

The most famous shipwreck caused by an iceberg was the sinking of the *Titanic* in 1912. An iceberg ripped a gigantic hole in the ship and over 1,500 people drowned.

The seas are filled with icebergs, especially in the North Atlantic. There are many thousands which float around. Some reach 500 feet above the water and are much larger beneath. Icebergs are such a great problem for ships that there is one agency whose full-time job is to watch icebergs and report their locations. Their work is something like airport controllers.

Some scientists believe icebergs could be used to help the dry areas in the world. They plan to pull a huge iceberg to the shore of a dry country. Water could then be pumped from the iceberg onto the shore. One scientist believes a large iceberg could inexpensively supply all of Los Angeles' water needs for one month.

There is no shortage of icebergs. They continue to break away from larger ice areas such as Iceland.

The sea is full of surprises and so is the rest of life. Some things like icebergs look great, but when you get too close they can hurt you.

There are some very nice people who tell us we really should not follow Jesus Christ. They laugh at us and say we are silly to be Christians. We need to watch out for this kind of teasing. It is as dangerous as an iceberg and we could end up with our faith sinking fast.

No matter who it is who makes fun of us, it makes far better sense to follow Jesus Christ.

"Holding faith, and a good conscience; which some having put away concerning faith have made shipwreck" (1 Tim. 1:19, KJV).

1. Where are most icebergs located?
2. What happened to the *Titanic*?
3. Has anyone ever made fun of your faith? If so, tell about it.

Keep our faith strong, dear Father.

eleven

The Mean Piranha

Once in a while you meet someone who is quick tempered and always grouchy. A few fish fit this picture exactly. None is meaner than the 18-inch beauty called the piranha.

It lives in South America and is always looking for a fight. A piranha doesn't merely pick on smaller fish. This little terror will attack a human, a horse, or a boat. They travel in schools and their tough teeth and rapid jaws can tear all the flesh from some unlucky animal in a few minutes.

A piranha *looks* like a friendly fish. It has pretty colors and is supposed to make good eating. However, if you try to catch one, you will not only need a metal hook but also a metal line.

Their teeth are as sharp as razors and move as quickly as buzz saws. If a visitor to the Amazon is canoeing and accidentally puts his hand in the water, he could lose all the skin. A piranha will bite your stick, pole, or oar and try to take it away from you.

Piranhas are not usually looking for people. Their diet normally consists of small fish. Sometimes they will attack birds on the water or an unsuspecting animal trying to cross the river. There are a few stories of piranhas killing people. But even so some people in Brazil swim in the same waters where piranhas live.

Most countries would like the piranha to stay in South America. However, pet shops have sold them, and the mean little monsters could get tossed into nearby rivers and lakes. The Florida area would be an excellent place for them to grow, so authorities keep watch. Ten years ago one piranha was found near Miami, but wardens don't expect any more.

Piranhas are a strange mixture of beauty and violence. On the outside their colors are beautiful, but on the inside there is a violent temper. When angered they become especially nasty.

People are too often the same way. We take time to comb our hair and make sure our clothes are neat, but sometimes we are hot tempered, demanding, and pushy on the inside.

We should be more concerned about our inward attitudes and the way we treat each other than the way we look. Jesus taught us to watch our hearts. It doesn't make any difference how good we look if we are mean inside.

"You try to look like saintly men, but underneath those pious robes of yours are hearts besmirched with every sort of hypocrisy and sin" (Matt. 23:28, TLB).

1. Where do piranhas live?
2. How big is a piranha?
3. Which is more important: how we look or how we act?

Please change our hearts and minds, Lord Jesus.

twelve

The Great Diver

It's a beautiful sight to see a flock of large gannets approaching. Have you ever seen one? Maybe you don't even know what a gannet is. It is a sea fowl, a member of the pelican family. Each one is about a yard long and they travel in groups of 10 to 100. They often search for schools of herring off the North Atlantic coast.

They will spot their prey about a half mile from shore. From a height of 75 feet the gannets begin their dive into the water. Almost like a hailstorm the entire flock races toward the water.

When the gannet hits the water and breaks through the surface, it causes a terrific splash. On impact water shoots 10 feet into the air. It's a spectacular sight to see 100 gannets smashing into the sea all at once.

This bird is almost as quick under water as it is in the air. The gannet swims with its wings half open and feet pumping hard. In a few seconds it catches a herring, eats it and begins its struggle toward the surface. If its dinner was hard to catch, it may go as far as 50 or more feet deep.

As the gannet comes up through the surface of the water, it flies away immediately. Its wings are so well formed and oiled that the water can't soak into them. Without waiting to dry they can fly straight out. The great diver soars into the sky and begins looking for another herring school. Before long it hopes to dive again.

If a gannet is to survive, it has to be strong. It must be able to protect itself on land, sea, and in the air. It leads a rugged life.

Maybe this is why gannets' parents leave the chicks on their own a little earlier than most birds. A week before a gannet chick can fly, the parents take off. Many times the young gannet will

This bird is almost as quick under water as it is in the air.

push itself into the water and float for a week. Without anything to eat, it begins to slim down until it is light enough to fly easily. The gannet then takes off, ready to struggle and win as a fantastic diver.

Every creature has to struggle. Whether it is a shark searching for food, a gannet looking for herring or a young person trying to grow up, all of us face struggles.

When a young person decides to be a Christian that struggle continues. People who don't understand might make fun of us. Those who want to live lawlessly might give us a hard time.

Sometimes the struggle isn't so tough and other times it's terrible. It helps to know the struggle is worth it. It makes more sense to follow Jesus Christ than any other way of life.

"Fight the good fight, lay hold on eternal life, whereunto thou

art also called, and hast professed a good profession before many witnesses" (1 Tim. 6:12, KJV).

1. What do gannets hunt?
2. Where do gannets hunt?
3. What do you feel is the hardest part about being a Christian? Explain.

We expect to struggle sometimes, Lord. But thank you for your help to overcome.

thirteen

Explorers of the Ocean

Would you like to visit the bottom of the ocean and see things no person has ever seen? Would you enjoy living in an underwater city?

Whatever we do in the future, we will be building on the knowledge, experience, and courage of people who first explored the sea. They did what others had only dreamed about. Some of the children of today might become the courageous sea explorers of tomorrow.

The most famous ocean pioneer of our time is Jacques-Yves Cousteau. His television specials have brought a knowledge of the ocean into millions of homes. However, Cousteau is far more than merely a television star.

In 1943 Cousteau joined Emile Gagnan to invent the famous aqualung. This allowed swimmers to carry air in a tank on their backs. As a result they could travel freely to 300 feet under water and stay there for hours. With the aqualung, people have been given a new freedom under the sea.

Another amazing sea explorer is Scott Carpenter. Before turning to the ocean, Carpenter was an astronaut. Today he is an aquanaut and the only person to have explored both outer space and the ocean depths. In 1962 Carpenter soared into space on the Apollo 7. Three years later, 1965, he traveled into the mysterious world of the ocean.

Carpenter became the first person to spend 30 days under water. He and other aquanauts lived in the 38-foot-long Sealab II.

During this time the explorers would leave the Sealab and investigate the underwater environment. They swam in water of only 50-degree temperatures.

Midway through their stay Carpenter was stung by the dorsal spines of a Red Scorpion fish. The pain was so intense it looked at first as if Carpenter would have to be taken to land. Fortunately he was able to complete the mission.

Men are not the only explorers of the deep. Dr. Sylvia Earle, a marine biologist, is involved in some amazing underwater experiments. Sylvia has worked so much in the sea that she has made personal friends with dolphins.

Someday we might be able to travel under the ocean. We will look at magnificent creatures, see the majestic formations, and maybe pick up some fascinating seashells. If we travel into the sea, it will be because of courageous explorers who went before us.

When we go to heaven, it will be because Jesus Christ has gone there first. He is now willing to lead us to that same heaven if we believe in Him.

"Even when walking through the dark valley of death, I will not be afraid, for you are close beside me, guarding, guiding all the way" (Ps. 23:4, TLB).

1. Who was the first astronaut and aquanaut?
2. Who invented the aqualung?
3. Who guides us to heaven? What do we need to do?

Thanks, Lord Jesus, for guiding us through life and death.

fourteen

The Gentle Giants

Giant Gray Whales don't have to be friendly. They are big enough to win a battle with most anyone or anything. If a whale crashes its 40-foot body into a small boat, everyone aboard could be killed. But for some reason this champion of the sea is usually gentle enough to let people pet him.

The Gray Whale hasn't always been kind. A hundred years

This champion of the sea is usually gentle enough to let people pet him.

ago it had a terrifying reputation. It was a hunted species and constantly in danger. At that time there were 25,000 Gray Whales in the ocean, but after 50 years of being hunted, their number was reduced to about 100. Then laws were passed to protect the large creature. And now there are again thousands of Gray Whales. Today, though, they are gentle giants.

Off the shores of southern California many people sail out to meet the Gray Whales. Thousands of others watch them from the ocean banks. Those in the boats have seen these creatures rise out of the water just a few hundred yards away. Air or spray comes spouting out of their backs and shoots 15 feet into the air.

More than once a Gray Whale has glided over to a boat and nuzzled close to its side. It will then hold still while the amazed onlookers pet the animal just as if it were a puppy. The whale will usually keep an eye on whoever touches it, but the creature acts just like an old friend.

Many thousands get to see the Gray Whales every year. Whales migrate from Baja in lower California to the Arctic seas and back again each year. The complete trip is over 12,000 miles. All along the way people line the banks to watch them. There are few better places to observe these travelers than the western coast of Vancouver Island.

The Gray Whale moves at a speed of almost 5 miles an hour, so it is slow enough to watch carefully. Each day he covers about 90 miles.

Each winter the whales return to balmy California where they have their baby calves. Baby Gray Whales are born with too little blubber to withstand the tough winters of the north.

A few people are still allowed to hunt the Gray Whale. They claim the creature is dangerous and will attack a boat of whalers. But almost all animals will attack those who try to kill them. This is because their lives are controlled by instincts and reactions which God built into them for protection.

God has made us different from the animals, though. He wants us to trust Him for protection, and He also wants us to protect others. We could try to show everyone how tough we are by being rude and nasty or beating on the kids who are smaller than we. But instead God wants us to be gentle, kind, and friendly. That's the way Jesus was. So we know that is the way He wants us to be.

"But when the Holy Spirit controls our lives he will produce

this kind of fruit in us: love, joy, peace, patience, kindness, good-ness, faithfulness, gentleness and self-control" (Gal. 5:22, TLB).

1. Where do Gray Whales migrate?
2. Why are their calves born in warm water?
3. Do you find it hard to be gentle? Explain.

We thank you, Lord, for the example you have given us for how we should live.

fifteen

Hermit Crabs

Our family was on a trip and it was getting dark. We had stopped at several motels, trying to find a room, but there were no vacancies. The later it got the more we began to worry. Maybe we wouldn't be able to find a place to stay.

I think that sometimes the Hermit crab must feel that way. In order to protect itself, this many-armed little creature must find an empty shell and move in. If it stays outside too long, an enemy will find it and eat crab for dinner.

This househunting presents some terrible problems. For one thing, the Hermit crab keeps growing and therefore needs to move to a bigger shell frequently. While he is moving, the crab is in great danger. Besides this, other Hermit crabs oftentimes want the same shell he is living in. He might have to put up a terrific fight to keep a roof over his head.

When the Hermit finds a house, immediately he gets ready for a possible attack on his new home. The crab's tail has two hooks with which he grabs onto the back of the shell. He then spreads his powerful claws across the opening, ready to tear at anything that dares intrude.

His is a hard life because he knows that his safety can't hold out forever. Sooner or later he will have to move again.

Some pet shops have Hermit crabs for sale, but usually they aren't easy to find. Most of them like to live under more than a hundred feet of water.

When a Hermit isn't househunting, it's on a search for food. Not a picky eater, it will feast on living or dead creatures.

Househunting can be fun or it can be frustrating. It's good to know that when we leave this earth, we won't have to search for a place to live. Jesus Christ has gone ahead of us and picked out a

In order to protect itself, this many-armed little creature must find an empty shell and move in.

tremendous place. When we believe in Jesus as our Savior, we can be sure there is a special home waiting for us in heaven.

"There are many homes up there where my Father lives, and I am going to prepare them for your coming" (John 14:2, TLB).

1. What do Hermit crabs eat?
2. How do they hang onto the shell?
3. What do you think a home in heaven will be like?

Dear Savior, thank you for preparing a place for us.

sixteen

Yesterday's Monsters

Most of the world has never been explored. There are places and creatures on our planet which no person has ever seen. In the near future we may see some tremendous surprises. Scientists only recently have started to look into the sea.

In 1976 a Navy vessel was anchored off the shores of Hawaii when something became caught in its lines. They captured the creature and found they had a twelve-foot, 1,500-pound shark. Scientists agree that this type of shark had never been seen before. They gave it the nickname of "Megamouth" because of its large mouth.

They believe Megamouth lives at a depth of 500 to 1,000 feet in the Pacific Ocean. Since people do not usually roam around that deep, one had never been caught before.

Another unusual fish is the coelacanth. The only way this fish had been seen before was as a fossil. Scientists had thought the coelacanth had not lived for 500 years. Then, one day, a coelacanth fish washed ashore in South Africa. It weighed 127 pounds and was 5 feet long. A few years later another one washed ashore, and then six more.

Where had the coelacanth been? Does it live some place where man does not go?

Do you have a good imagination? A larva is a tiny creature just born or hatched. Scientists found an eel larva near the Cape of Good Hope. This newborn larva was over 5 feet long! How big would that eel have gotten as an adult? It could have reached 90 feet.

Maybe you aren't in a hurry to see a huge sea monster. Think about a small one. When a fur seal was caught off the shores of California, a small fish was found in its stomach. No man has ever seen this fish swimming in the water. Seals can find fish we know nothing about.

Many centuries ago Job described a terrible sea monster. Smoke flowed from this monster's nose. Fire shot out of its mouth. No sword could stop it, and a hook certainly could not catch it.

Did Job really see this amazing monster? There are creatures deep in the sea that no man has yet seen.

God has put an amazing world together. Maybe we will get to explore more of its wonders.

Job's monster:

"When he sneezes, the sunlight sparkles like lightning across the vapor droplets. His eyes glow like sparks. Fire leaps from his mouth. Smoke flows from his nostrils, like steam from a boiling pot that is fired by dry rushes. Yes, his breath would kindle coals—flames leap from his mouth" (Job 40:18-21, TLB).

1. What is megamouth?
2. Would you like to explore the deep ocean? Why?
3. Do you think Job really saw this monster?

The world you have made is filled with wonders, God.

seventeen

Poisonous Plants

There are some plants in the sea which are bright and beautiful. Because of their rich colors, we might think it would be fun to pick them. But it wouldn't. Some of them carry deadly poisons and actually eat animals.

One of the most dangerous plants is the Urchin or pincushion. In the water the Urchin looks harmless, but if you touch one of its many long needles, you could be in trouble. Deep-sea divers stay away from them because they understand the danger. An Urchin needle could break off in a person's flesh and make him terribly sick.

Living in the same neighborhood as the Urchin, you might find the colorful Sea Anemone. These plants are so gorgeous you might be tempted to pick one. If you grab this little plant, you will probably end up with a paralyzed hand.

Anemones don't always wait to be touched, though. If a fish swims nearby, the anemone can shoot out an arm and sting the creature. This way the fish is paralyzed and captured, and the plant can then eat the fish.

Despite the strong poison of the anemone, there is one fish that isn't afraid of it. This is the attractive Striped Anemone fish. This fish has developed a resistance to the anemone sting. While other fish are killed, this creature can be near the anemone without suffering the slightest injury.

Life has some real dangers for people, too. We may not be stung by an anemone or stuck by a pincushion, but there are plenty of things that could hurt us.

God understands those things which make us afraid. He wants to be our companion and help us to feel peace. God wants to guide and protect us because we belong to Him. It's great to have someone watching over us.

"But all who listen to me shall live in peace and safety, unafraid" (Prov. 1:33, TLB).

1. How does an urchin attack?
2. What fish doesn't fear the anemone?
3. All of us have fears. What fear would you like God to help you with?

Thank you for peace, God.

eighteen

Escape Hatch

Submarines have always been dangerous and many men have lost their lives in them. An early experimenter named Day proved that he could stay in a submarine for 24 hours at a depth of 30 feet. However, in 1774 on his second try, Day drowned.

Modern submarines are not without their problems. In 1963 the nuclear-powered *Thresher* sank 200 miles off the Boston coast. It plunged 8,400 feet and all the crew was lost.

In 1968 the submarine *Scorpion* sank near the Azores in the Atlantic. None of its men could be rescued.

If a submarine drops too far into the sea, its metal cannot stand the pressure and will collapse. Engineers are working to build stronger submarines that are able to resist this pressure.

What happens if a submarine drops a few hundred feet and for some reason cannot come up again? How can the crew be rescued? Or can they?

One way to escape from a submarine is to use the escape hatch. Several sailors can stand in this little room and gradually let sea water in. When the hatch is full they then open the lid and float up to the surface.

Just before the men are covered with the water and open the lid, they take a deep breath. As they rise to the surface they slowly let the air out. It is called "blow and go." The sailor will travel a hundred feet or more in a few seconds.

The Navy also has special "lungs" or air bags which can be used. They allow the person to breathe as he goes up.

As more people go deeper into the ocean, better rescue devices are necessary. People must be able to escape from tremendous depths.

Scientists have now developed special rescue submarines.

These submarines go down thousands of feet. When they find the vessel in trouble, the rescue ship locks itself onto the submarine. After it is locked the crew can simply climb from one submarine into the other and escape.

Before escape hatches and rescue submarines were invented, life under water was much more dangerous. I'm sure that each person who went under water in a submarine was concerned about a way to escape in case of trouble.

God has given all of us the same hope for our lives. Sometimes life can be terribly hard. Often we are tempted to do wrong things. We know we shouldn't do these things, but we feel that it's too hard to say no to them.

Don't give in, though. Don't do the sin that tempts you. God will give you a way to keep from doing it. He has promised an escape hatch.

"He will show you how to escape temptation's power so that you can bear up patiently against it" (1 Cor. 10:13, TLB).

1. What happened to the USS *Thresher*?
2. How can one escape from a submarine?
3. What sins have tempted you? How did you escape?

Thank you for escape hatches, heavenly Father.

nineteen

Sweetlips

Some people's names tell us what they look like. Someone might be nicknamed "Curly" because his hair is curly or "Slim" because he's tall and thin. "Lefty" and "Red" are some other common nicknames.

In the sea world we have given odd names to many creatures. Usually these names describe the appearance or the behavior of the animal.

We don't know who first called a certain fish "sweetlips," but if you could see this fish, you would understand why. A sweetlip naturally has large lips. The fish will leave its lips open and allow the little fish called wrasse to eat from its mouth. The wrasse eats parasites and diseased tissue. It does sweetlips a big favor.

Can you guess how a surgeonfish got its name? It carries small knives. Actually they are sharp spines, but they can cut like a razor. There are 100 different kinds of surgeonfish and the strangest is the yellow surgeon. Their spines have jackknives. These knives pop out and then go back into hiding.

Maybe you enjoy hard names. Try pronouncing humuhumunukunukuapuaa. This little creature lives near Hawaii. Its more popular name is the triggerfish.

You need to see the hatchet fish to understand how it got its name. A small fish, it has a tiny tail and a large body. It looks like something that could chop wood.

Various kinds of sharks look much alike except for one. The hammerhead shark is different. It has a wide, flat nose. Its eyes are far apart at each end of its nose. Despite its strange appearance, the hammerhead is still a dangerous creature.

Names are labels. We would be at a loss if we didn't have them. Most of the names we have heard we have already forgotten. There are just too many to remember.

Yet one name stands out above all others. The name Jesus is special. It means Savior and applies to the Son of God. His name describes what He is. Jesus is our Savior. His life, death, and resurrection have made it possible for us to live with Him forever.

Someday everyone will bow down before the name of Jesus Christ.

"That at the name of Jesus Christ every knee shall bow in heaven and on earth and under the earth" (Phil. 2:10, TLB).

1. How did the surgeonfish get its name?
2. What helps sweetlips?
3. Why is the name of Jesus important?

There is one name above all others. We thank you for the meaning of your name, Jesus.

twenty

Slow Snails

The next time you go to a restaurant, ask for an order of escargot. If they have it, you will soon get a plate full of piping hot snails. Millions of people enjoy them every year. Those who eat snail insist they have a delicious taste.

Snails are on one hand the friend of man and on the other they are enemies.

There is no shortage of snails. They are found in practically every part of the world, including salt water, fresh water and dry land. Some are shaped in a left-handed position and others swirl to the right.

Snails aren't great parents, but their babies don't seem to mind. The mother will deposit her eggs into a two-to-four-inch hole. She will cover the 20 eggs and rub until the spot is smooth. The mother then leaves and never returns.

A month later the eggs hatch. The new snails are entirely on their own and must find food for themselves.

Snails are on one hand the friend of man and on the other they are enemies. Snails give us food, clean up nature, and furnish medicine. However, snails also ruin crops, pollute water, and make animals and people sick.

The poky snail looks harmless, but clams don't think so. A snail will attach itself to the shell of a clam and slowly begin to drill through. When it reaches the soft clam the snail slowly sucks it up.

Snails have reputations for being almost as slow as a rock. It is true that they don't seem to get too excited. We don't see snails rushing around.

Many snails refuse to travel if the weather is hot. Land snails often stay still if it's too wet. When they take a nap it may last a while. They sleep for days and many hibernate all winter. A few pull back into their shell and sleep for four years. They try hard to avoid too much excitement.

Most of the time we wouldn't want to be snails. However, once in a while it would come in handy. We would be better off if we were as slow as snails at becoming angry.

We all know some people who seem to get angry easily and often. The Bible tells us to keep from getting angry too quickly. It isn't good for anyone if we are a "hothead."

"It is better to be slow tempered than famous; it is better to have self-control than to control an army" (Prov. 16:32, TLB).

1. What is escargot?
2. What kind of parents are snails?
3. Are you a "hothead" or slow to anger? Explain.

Help us control our temper, Holy Spirit.

twenty-one

Can Fish Breathe?

People have a few gigantic problems with living in the sea. One problem is the pressure from the water. Most submarines will crush like pop cans if they go down too far. The other problem is air. How are people going to breathe under water? Presently they can carry their own supply of air, but they can't swim freely like a fish. How can a fish breathe under water? Or do they breathe?

Fish have special body parts called gills. They are located just behind the head. A fish takes water into its mouth. The water is then forced through the gills. After it passes through the gills, the water is released by openings on its side next to its head. If you pick up a fish, you can see the openings.

While the water passes over the gills the fish breathes. Its gills take oxygen out of the water and it goes into the bloodstream. The gills also release carbon dioxide which is carried outside the body.

This is a simple process for the fish. It works just as smoothly for them as air does for us.

It may be possible for man to do this in the future. Suppose we could put on a helmet that allowed us to breathe right from the sea? If scientists could build mechanical gills on the helmet, we could take in oxygen and release carbon dioxide from water.

If this were possible, people could swim freely without carrying an air tank and surfacing when it runs out. This wouldn't solve all our problems in the sea, but it would be a big step.

It must take a rich imagination for God to create all the marvels of nature. He has given animals special abilities that we barely understand.

Have you ever wondered how people will breathe in heaven? Will there be any air? Will we breathe something special which we have never heard of? Maybe we will live without any need to breathe.

God has created an amazing world. He has planned an even more fascinating heaven.

"For our earthly bodies, the ones we have now that can die, must be transformed into heavenly bodies that cannot perish but will live forever" (1 Cor. 15:53, TLB).

1. How do gills work?
2. How could people "breathe" under water?
3. What do you think heaven is like?

Thanks for promising us an amazing tomorrow, God.

twenty-two

Underwater Carpenters

Few animals have as much imagination as the North American beaver. Although they don't live in the sea, they do live in water. By building wooden dams they back up water, making beautiful ponds and reservoirs.

Beavers are hard workers. With their tough front teeth, sure hands, and webbed hind feet they make most of what they need.

They begin as carpenters. Using their hatchet-like front teeth, the beaver cuts down trees as large as three and a half feet around. They eat the bark but drag off the wood to build their excellent lodges.

A beaver lodge serves as a dam and in many areas helps both animals and people. The pond created by the dam controls floods and holds water until it is needed.

Over the past 200 years people have killed off millions of beaver. Some scientists believe there are more floods today because we have less beaver to control the waterways.

The doors to a beaver lodge are found beneath the water. Beavers dive under the water and come up inside their snug living room. The lodge has several entrances and exits.

Beavers are not content just to build a home; they are also careful to keep it in good repair. Each fall they patch and remodel it. Sticks are added to any sagging areas and fresh mud is packed into any holes. Because of this careful work, beaver lodges last for many years through tough winters. Some beaver homes are 100 feet long and have lasted for 200 years.

As busy as beavers are, they manage to include their family in their work. A beaver selects one wife for life. Mother and father beaver are careful to train their babies (called kits) for two or three years before letting them go on their own.

To protect his family from danger the beaver has a special signal. If the father thumps his tail loudly against the ground, it means "dive immediately." The kit who learns his lessons well does not take time to look around or question. The thump sends him heading for the water and he drops like a rock.

Beavers care about their kits, and the kits that obey their parents often live long enough to start their own beaver lodge.

In this way beavers are much like people. The children who grow up obeying their parents find life the safest and even the happiest. Rebellious children usually have a harder time.

God knew this and gave us good instructions. Children who obey their parents begin their life in a strong, healthy way.

"Children, obey your parents; this is the right thing to do because God has placed them in authority over you" (Eph. 6:1, TLB).

1. When do beavers usually repair their lodge?
2. What are beaver children called?
3. Name something you have learned from your parents.

Thank you, God, for giving us parents.

twenty-three

The Alligator Snapper

There is no need to go to sea looking for a water-loving turtle. In the United States the alligator snapper lives in fresh water. This turtle likes a warm climate so he normally waddles around in the southern states.

Snappers grow to a large size. The record is probably 236 pounds. On the average, though, they stay closer to 35-50 pounds. Their length is about sixteen inches.

The alligator snapper is fascinating. It has a reputation as a fisherman. It isn't fast or known for being clever since it likes to rest in about six feet of water and take life easy.

This snapper has a small pinkish piece of skin inside the lower jaw. It wiggles enough to make a tempting sight to unsuspecting fish. As soon as the prey comes close to check it out, the turtle merely makes a fast snap, and has a meal. It then opens its mouth and waits for another curious visitor.

Alligator snappers aren't completely lazy, however. If the fish bait trick isn't working, snappers will search for food. A few snails or mussels will tide them over until the next fish. As with other turtles the alligator snapper isn't a big eater for its size. But, then, it doesn't burn up calories like a jogger, either.

Turtle is frequently eaten by North Americans and the snapper is our number-one choice. Five tons are caught annually in the Mississippi Valley. In some restaurants turtle meat is served as a delicacy, and many southern folks, in particular, enjoy turtle meat.

It isn't unusual to see small snapping turtles trying to cross the highways of America. Many scientists are baffled by this dangerous trick. Turtles are basically water creatures. What odd urge takes them to highways? Their movement does not seem to be connected to age or even dry seasons. Yet many take up this dry land journey and are killed on the roads.

Whether it's the snapper killed on the highway or the fish that is lured by a funny pink bait into the turtle's mouth, both find out too late that they have made a mistake.

People often fall for Satan's tricks the same way. The devil is busy trying to get us to do something evil. However, Satan is clever. Many times he gets us to follow him before we realize it. Satan may be better at trapping people than the snapper is at fishing.

There are two good ways to learn Satan's tricks. First, we need to know the warnings in the Bible. Second, we need to listen to parents who care about us.

"Put on all of God's armor so that you will be able to stand safe against all strategies and tricks of Satan" (Eph. 6:11, TLB).

1. Where do alligator snappers live?
2. How do they catch fish?
3. How are young people tricked into doing evil?

Guard us from life's traps, Holy Spirit.

twenty-four

Drinking Water

Water can be dangerous. For centuries men have known this and have selected water that has been filtered through streams or taken from high lakes. Yet only during the past 100 years have we realized how harmful water can be.

In 1892 Dr. Robert Kick proved the difference between filtered and non-filtered water. He knew that people in Hamburg, Germany, were contracting the dreaded cholera by drinking the city water. Drinking water was carrying terrible bacteria which could not be seen but yet were killing people.

Today water is carefully treated to protect us from disease. Years ago, and in some places now, water had to be boiled before anyone could drink or cook with it.

In many cities more is done to the water than merely destroying bacteria. Chemicals called coagulents are added to take the color out of drinking water. It pulls the color together and makes it settle on the bottom.

The chemicals often leave the water hard and foul tasting. To get rid of this side effect, something similar to lime soda is added. This softens the water. It is then run rapidly through sand filters to improve the taste and color.

Water doesn't seem hard for most of us to get. If we turn on a faucet, water automatically comes out. We don't usually worry if water will come or if it contains dangerous bacteria.

However, many people in the world still have trouble getting good, safe water. Some people must travel for miles to get it, while others carry water in jars on their heads. These jars can weigh 50 pounds when full.

Jesus cares about our physical needs of food, clothing and water, but He is even more concerned about giving us peace with God. The person who believes in Jesus Christ has something even more important than water—he has eternal life.

The woman who came to a well in Samaria was one who had to carry water some distance on her head. Most likely she was careful not to waste any.

When Jesus met this lady He talked to her about water, because it was on her mind. Then he turned the conversation to something more important. He talked to her about living forever.

"If you only knew what a wonderful gift God has for you, and who I am, you would ask me for some living water" (John 4:10, TLB).

1. How is drinking water treated?
2. Who discovered cholera bacteria in water?
3. What does "living water" mean?

Thank you, God, for life that does not end.

twenty-five

The Knights of the Sea

The earth's waters are filled with unique characters. Otters are clowns, dolphins are friends, and oysters are jewelers. However, there is no character quite like the hard-shell, armored knight—the lobster.

Most of us don't live near lobsters, so we know little of how they get around. I think it is fair to say there is no odder creature in the sea.

Lobsters seem to do everything either backwards or upside down. The lobster's brain is in its throat. It tastes with its feet and hears with its legs. After a lobster has swallowed, it chews its food with teeth inside its stomach.

If trouble comes close, our friend doesn't run away in normal style. Lobsters will rapidly back away. Even though it looks slow, it can cover ten feet of dry land in one second.

A lobster is like a rhinoceros in that it is nearsighted and hot tempered. Since it isn't always sure what is going on, it attacks with terror if anything gets close.

When it is young, a lobster isn't at all afraid to pick a fight with another lobster and then eat it. As it grows older it seems to give up cannibalism.

Not only is it tough in a fight, but a lobster is great at recovering. If it has a claw or a leg torn off, it can grow the part back. It may take a while, but it can be done even after the lobster has lost a large section of its body.

Often a lobster will have one slender claw and the other will be heavy. It uses the smaller one to lunge out and grab an enemy.

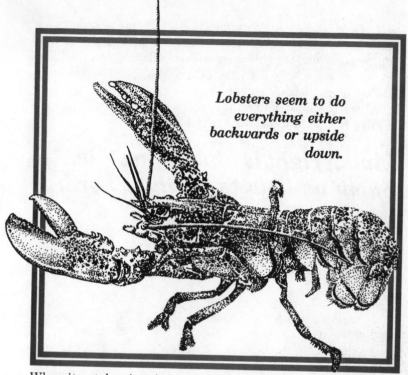

Lobsters seem to do everything either backwards or upside down.

When it catches its victim, it then lays the big one on him.

Usually the knight of the sea prefers to hide during the day. At night it climbs out from behind a rock and looks for supper.

A lobster needs all the armor it can get. From its first day this creature leads a hard life. Only one in 10,000 lobsters will ever grow up. When an elderly 25-pound lobster is caught, the fisherman can see the many marks and scars on its shell. These are evidence of the many battles it has survived.

Some days many of us wish we had a tough set of armor. When you play kickball or football, a good, hard suit would come in handy.

There is also an invisible armor that will help us! The Bible tells us that this world can be mean and evil sometimes. All of us feel how cruel life is once in a while. We can protect ourselves by putting on a suit of armor called right living. By doing what is good and right we keep from being captured by terrible sin.

The person who is determined to do what is right does not have to be afraid. He has his armor on.

"So quit the evil deeds of darkness and put on the armor of right living, as we who live in the daylight should! Be decent and

65

true in everything you do so that all can approve your behavior. Don't spend your time in wild parties and getting drunk or in adultery and lust, or fighting or jealousy" (Rom. 13:12, 13, TLB).

1. How does a lobster escape?
2. Where is a lobster's brain?
3. Why is it hard to do what is right?

Living right is always in style. Show us how to do this, Lord.

twenty-six

Flying Fish

Nature is amazing. A penguin is a bird, but it doesn't fly. An ostrich is a bird, but it's too large to leave the ground. But more strange than this, there are fish that act like birds.

Actually there are a number of fish that fly. To be more accurate, they sail through the air. The manta ray weighs a ton and a half but glides above the water. Blue marlins and dolphins can leave the sea to do beautiful arches.

Flying fish do not stay in the air for long, but they are fast and can cover a large distance.

The most famous flying fish is a small creature that can be found around the West Indies. If you ever get there, ask the waiter for flying fish pie. You may enjoy it.

Fish do not fly exactly as birds. Their motions are closer to the flying squirrel. They push themselves out of the water by rapidly wiggling their tails. This propeller gets them airborne and then their sailing fins take over.

Flying fish do not stay in the air for long, but they are fast and can cover a large distance. They have been timed at 35 miles an hour. If they stay in the air for 13 seconds, they can travel 600 feet, the length of 2 football fields. This means a flying fish can sail over twice as fast as most children could run that same distance.

Few of us have seen a flying fish. In fact, some people used to think they were just a myth. However, flying fish are caught and eaten in great numbers.

Dolphins believe in flying fish. When they land, the dolphin is often there, waiting to eat them.

We shouldn't be surprised. God's world is amazing. There are many fascinating things our Creator has made which we have never even seen. He is the Creator of variety, splendor, and imagination.

When He works in people's lives, God is the same Creator. He might want to do things in your life you have never imagined. His plan for your future may be more spectacular than all the creatures of the sea.

"No mere man has ever seen, heard or imagined what wonderful things God has ready for those who love the Lord" (1 Cor. 2:9, TLB).

1. Name a fish that "flies."
2. How fast can a flying fish travel?
3. Name some ways God uses people.

Thank you for a fascinating tomorrow, Father.

twenty-seven

Run Cars with Water?

"Don't forget to water the car." Can you imagine a father saying this to his oldest child? Don't laugh. It isn't as strange as it sounds. Some dedicated scientists believe there's a possibility of running cars on water instead of gas. Since the world is 70 percent water, it would be a lot easier to get fuel.

For hundreds of years many people have believed this could be done. The famous science fiction writer, Jules Verne, predicted that some of our heat and light would come from water.

It wouldn't be hard to do, either. Water consists of two parts hydrogen and one part oxygen. Hydrogen can burn just like other gases. All we would have to do is separate the hydrogen from the water and then burn it. We could pour water into our car and with the help of a simple machine, the hydrogen would be automatically separated and burned. This sounds easy, and in some ways it is.

Hydrogen power is not new. Almost 45 years ago a blimp, the Hindenburg, was filled with hydrogen. It exploded over Lakehurst, New Jersey, in 1937. In our lifetime hydrogen has also been used to power rocket ships and build powerful bombs.

God made man with great intelligence. There are many things we have not yet solved, but there are so many problems we've already conquered.

The biggest problem with using hydrogen to run our car is the danger involved. Hydrogen can be highly explosive. It must be controlled.

Some of our fear of hydrogen is going away. The soap in your bathroom was probably made by using hydrogen. If you use margarine or shortening, it may have been produced with the help of hydrogen. One scientist believes we will soon run our kitchen stoves on water or hydrogen.

During the next 25 years we might see airplanes, automobiles, trucks and trains running with water as the fuel. As oil, coal, and natural gas become harder to get, we may need to find other forms of energy.

Life changes quickly. Just 100 years ago there were no airplanes and horses were used instead of cars. No one had a radio then and certainly there were no television sets.

The next one hundred years may be even more exciting. Don't be surprised if someday you tell your son, "Be sure to put a gallon of water in the car."

God created a fantastic world which overflows with good things. He is happy to see us use these resources and to use them safely. Who knows what amazing things might come tomorrow.

"The intelligent man is always open to new ideas. In fact, he looks for them" (Prov. 18:15, TLB).

1. How can a car run on water?
2. What is the main problem with hydrogen?
3. Name some good things God has created.

Thank you, God, for being so generous to us.

twenty-eight

Pirate Bird

The seas used to be filled with dangerous pirates who attacked and robbed ships. In the early 1700s, many fortunes were taken by crooks armed with swords, pistols, and blaring cannons.

Nature is still filled with its share of pirates. Instead of finding food for themselves, some creatures would rather wait and steal it from someone else.

One famous pirate of the sea is the skua. This large sea gull is found around the cold shores of the Arctic. Its close relatives live in different parts of the world.

If the skua wants to, it can work. It fishes and has other ways of collecting food. The problem, though, is that the skua does not want to work. It would rather steal.

This pirate bird keeps its eyes on the smaller sea gulls as they hunt for fish in the sea. When the smaller sea gull dives for a fish and snatches it from the water, the skua moves in like Blackbeard the pirate. The skua chases after the smaller gull and frightens it. In a hurry to get away, the gull will drop its fish. Like a jet plane the skua drops down and catches the prize in mid-air.

Many of us have someone in our neighborhood who reminds us of the skua. This person is mean and pushy. Sometimes he takes things from the younger or smaller kids. Instead of waiting his turn, he breaks into line and acts ugly. He acts like a playground pirate.

We may not be able to change people like this. However, we certainly don't have to become like them.

We can still be kind when others are nasty. We can tell the truth when other people lie. We can absolutely refuse to steal even if everyone else steals.

71

God wants us to do many great things, but He never wants us to become pirates.

"If anyone is stealing he must stop it and begin using those hands of his for honest work so he can give to others in need" (Eph. 4:28, TLB).

1. Where does the pirate bird live?
2. How does it steal?
3. Have you ever tried to get even with a school pirate? Should you? Explain how you feel.

Teach us to give instead of taking, Holy Spirit.

twenty-nine

Ghost Crabs

If you get near the Chesapeake Bay, you will want to spend some time crabbing. Crabs are fascinating creatures that walk sideways, have eyes on the ends of antennae, have eight legs and one or two large claws. When you handle them, be careful. Crabs are quick and their pinch can be painful.

The Chesapeake Bay is excellent for crabs because of its brackish water. It is a right mixture of fresh and salt water. If, because of storms, the water is churned up and the Bay gets too much of either, less crabs are born.

Crabs are often caught because they become foolish. If you place a chicken neck or wing on a string and drop it into the water, a crab will start nibbling on it. When it begins to eat, you slowly pull the string toward the surface. Usually the crab will be so busy eating it will not notice it is being lifted up.

When the bait and crab are near the top, you slowly put a net under the crab. If you're careful you will have fresh crab for dinner.

When we were at the Bay, our family caught blue crabs, but there are many different varieties. One of the strangest is the fiddler crab. It has one large claw, and some people think it looks like it is playing a violin.

When a fiddler crab is looking for a mate, it merely waves its huge claw in the air. When the female sees the claw, the male waves harder and faster. He looks like a child screaming on the playground.

While crabs make a good meal, the food they eat doesn't sound nearly as appetizing. They live mainly off dead plants and animals.

The best times to catch crabs in the Chesapeake is during

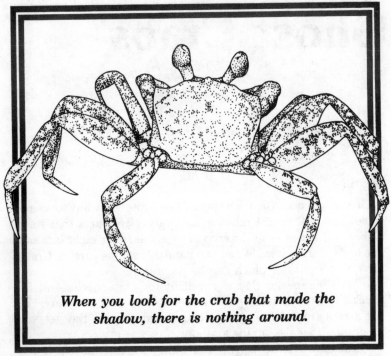

When you look for the crab that made the shadow, there is nothing around.

spring and summer. When fall hits they move out toward the deep center. They evidently want to get away from the cold surface. It is also easier to find oxygen in the deep water during winter.

Not all crabs live in the water. The strange ghost crab makes its home in a hole on the beach.

Ghost crabs are fitted well for living on a sandy, rocky beach. The color of the crab blends in perfectly. Some days you can see a small shadow hurrying swiftly past your feet. When you look for the crab that made the shadow, there is nothing around. At first it gives you a funny feeling to see shadows dashing across the beach.

We often see God the same way we see ghost crabs. Without really seeing Him, we can see what He has done. We look at the sky, the trees, the animals, the rivers and we know He is there. It is like seeing His shadow without really seeing Him.

When we see the flag flying, we know the wind is around. When we see the moving shadow, we know there must be a ghost crab. When we see our fantastic world, we know our Creator and God must be there.

"Since earliest times men have seen the earth and sky and all God made, and have known of his existence and great eternal power" (Rom. 1:20, TLB).

1. Where can you catch blue crabs?
2. Why is one kind of crab called a ghost crab?
3. What do you think are two of God's loveliest creations?

The world around us points to a living God. We thank you, Lord, for it.

thirty

The Underwater Saw

This creature looks more like a science fiction fish than a real one. However, the sawfish is alive and roaming the wide-open seas.

A sawfish looks like most other large, 12-to-18-foot-long sea creatures. The big difference is a huge double-edged saw where other fish have a nose. This saw alone can be as long as a full-grown man.

Its nose doesn't just *look* like a saw, it really *is* one. Each small edge is as sharp as a razor. It cuts through most things in just a few seconds.

Practically every fish has teeth, fins, and a rudder-like tail. That's normal. However, the sawfish is the only one with this carpenter's tool instead of a nose.

The sawfish uses its strange feature in at least two ways. Sometimes it digs into the ground if it is looking for something special. More often the saw is used to prepare dinner. A sawfish will swim into a school of small fish and rapidly begin to saw away. In a minute it has sliced up a large meal and begins to eat.

Old fishermen used to claim the sawfish would attack a wooden boat and try to cut a hole in the bottom. It may not be likely, but it is possible.

A few times sawfish have attacked people. When this happens the person has little chance. Even a baby sawfish can do tremendous injury. Sawfish almost never attack people, so there is little to fear. Marked swimming areas are safe.

One group of people make special use of a sawfish saw. When some Thailand people catch one, they sacrifice the saw as an offering in their temple.

A sawfish saw is an attempt to please God with a gift, but it isn't the one God most wants. The Bible says there is something God would rather have than a sacrifice. God would rather see us show mercy to each other.

Mercy means helping others. It means we don't hurt people. Mercy means we feed the needy or give shelter when it's necessary. Mercy means we become friends to the kid who is lonely and shy. Mercy means we don't say things to hurt someone's feelings.

Mercy is a word that covers many areas. Always it has to do with the way we treat people.

We can be glad God didn't ask us to go collect sawfish saws. However, He did ask us to care about others. Sometimes that's hard, too.

"It isn't your sacrifices and your gifts I want—I want you to be merciful" (Matt. 9:13, TLB).

1. How long are sawfish saws?
2. How does the sawfish use its saw?
3. What does God ask of us more than gifts and sacrifices?

Teach us to help and not to hurt, dear God.

thirty-one

Life in a Seashell

Who wants to spend his life stuck between two shells with nothing to do but watch the ocean run by? That kind of existence seems mighty dull to us land people. However, in the opinion of a simple shell scallop, his life is fast, exciting, and dangerous.

A scallop's life is different from his relatives, the clam and the oyster. To begin with, a scallop can move and do it quickly. This creature has its own jet-propulsion system. When in danger the scallop swallows water rapidly and then pushes it out again. This motion moves him swiftly away from an enemy. Not only can he get around, but he can also control the direction he travels.

Not every day is an exciting adventure, though. The scallop likes to sit still and eat the tiny food particles or plankton that float by. His life goes on peaceably until the scallop smells a scoundrel. Starfish like to pry open scallop shells and eat them for supper. So when our shelled friend picks up the starfish scent, it scurries away to the bottom of the sea.

When you first see a scallop, you might think it would be difficult to catch. Scallops have a terrific collection of small blue eyes. Some have as many as one hundred tiny eyes dotted along the opening in their shells.

Despite the large number of eyes, though, they don't see very well. They merely recognize suspicious looking shadows and smells that tell them danger is near.

Many of us have seen scallop shells without even knowing it. The shell on the Shell Oil Company sign is that of a scallop.

If you are looking for a good-paying job, maybe you could

make eyeglasses for scallops. Each scallop will need at least fifty pair. Maybe a few will order a hundred contact lenses! It's hard to imagine someone having so many eyes and yet hardly being able to see.

Worse than this, though, sometimes those of us who have good strong eyes still can't see very well. That's what Jesus taught us. We often do not notice when someone else needs help. Sometimes we don't see how we hurt our parents, brother, sister, or someone else. It is easy to look and yet not see at all.

There are people all around us who need someone to be kind, gentle, and caring. Jesus taught us to open our eyes and see how many ways we can help.

"Say not ye, There are yet four months, and then cometh harvest? Behold, I say unto you, Lift up your eyes, and look at the fields; for they are white already to harvest" (John 4:35, KJV).

1. How many eyes do some scallops have?
2. What do scallops eat?
3. What needs do you see around you?

Teach us to keep our eyes open, Lord Jesus.

thirty-two

What Killed the Dead Sea?

People who can't swim could still enjoy a good day on the lake if they could travel to Israel and wade into the Dead Sea. Their dreams of swimming and floating would come true there. All they have to do is lie down flat on the water and they won't sink. The water is so dense with minerals that people will not go under.

The Dead Sea is one of the most amazing bodies of water in the world. Normally the ocean contains 3.5 percent minerals. But this lake measures over 25 percent. That is why it is often called the Salt Sea.

This lake is one of the few which has polluted itself. It receives its water from the Jordan River and a number of small streams (six million gallons a day). These steadily feed the body of water, but there is no outlet. Water can only come in. The only way it can escape is by evaporation.

Since water can't run uphill there is no channel to release liquid. The lake is situated at 1,292 feet below sea level. This is the lowest level in the entire world.

Fortunately there isn't much rainfall into the sea—only two to four inches a year. If there were a large amount, it would cause floods.

The Dead Sea is large and gradually growing deeper. It is 53 miles long and ranges three to ten miles wide. At its deepest point it sinks 1,300 feet. In the past 70 years it has grown 20 feet deeper.

Located in a hot desert region, the evaporation process keeps sapping the lake. During the summer months the temperature reaches 140 degrees. The winter does allow the thermometer to drop below 80 degrees.

As the water escapes into the air, it leaves the minerals behind. They continue to saturate the lake and settle on the bottom. A visitor can see salt lying in the water and can pick it up by the handful.

The Dead Sea will not always be dead. The Bible tells us fish will someday dance in the water and fishermen will cast their nets. Its damaging salt will be removed and the water will become pure (see Ezek. 47:7-10).

God is able to make the dead come to life. It's one of His wonderful powers. He even takes dead people and makes them live forever.

Those who believe in Jesus Christ and die are promised a new life. God has the final power over death.

"Jesus told her, 'I am the one who raises the dead and gives them life again. Anyone who believes in me, even though he dies like everyone else, shall live again' " (John 11:25, TLB).

1. Why is the Dead Sea dead?
2. Describe a swim in the Dead Sea.
3. Will you live after death? Why?

Lord Jesus, you have overcome death.

thirty-three

The Hammerhead Shark

Sharks aren't as dangerous as most people think. Every year more deaths are caused by bee stings or lightning than by these toothy creatures. While we certainly should respect them, generally a shark will swim away from us.

One of the sharks we need to respect is the odd-looking hammerhead. Most sharks have a fairly pointed face, but not this creature. His nose is flat and stretches as much as three feet across. The hammerhead's eyes are at each end of this structure. A close relative of his is called the shovelhead.

Hammerheads love to eat stingrays. Other sharks enjoy them, too, but a stingray can generally fight. Normally, a stingray will try to sting a shark in the eyes. With the hammerhead it's a different story. Its eyes are set so far apart from its mouth that the stingray can't defend itself. One hammerhead was found with 50 stings in its back. It had paid a heavy price for its favorite meal.

Sharks have two strong senses which help them hunt. Their ability to smell and hear is outstanding. If blood is spilled in the water, its scent can be picked up from miles away by a shark. Though unable to see the goal, it can follow the smell to the exact location.

Scientists are now discovering that sharks are almost as good at hearing. A tape recording of fish struggling was played in the

Their ability to smell and hear is outstanding.

water, and in a few minutes two sharks showed up. They did this without the help of a scent.

The person who is really asking for trouble is the one who spearfishes in the evening in waters that sharks are known to visit. The first reason is because sharks aim for shallow shores in the evening. And the second is because a person in the water with a wiggling, bloody fish on this spear is practically calling for a shark.

We have little to fear from sharks. Most of the time they are happy to stay in their own area and likewise they want us to stay in ours.

The smart swimmer finds out where the dangerous spots are and he stays away from them. He also learns what is foolish to do in the water and does not do it.

Basically, those are the rules of life. We learn early what is dangerous and we try to avoid it. Those who live recklessly often get hurt.

That's part of the reason why God gave us the Bible. He

wanted to keep us from getting hurt. God gave us some guidelines. He said not to do this and watch out for that. When we don't listen, we get into trouble.

Pick up the Bible as a book of help. If we listen to its warnings, life goes much better.

"I am not writing about these things to make you ashamed, but to warn and counsel you as beloved children" (1 Cor. 4:14, TLB).

1. What is a hammerhead's favorite meal?
2. Why is spearfishing dangerous in certain places?
3. Tell about a warning from the Bible.

Thank you, God, for the helpful "stop" signs.

thirty-four

Seals Go to the Mountains

One of the South Pole's more interesting creatures is the weddell seal. James Weddell made a drawing of one in 1823. They are not always the cute little circus performers we are used to seeing. Some of these deep-sea divers weigh 900 pounds.

Their underwater abilities are the envy of man. The weddell seal can stop breathing for 30 minutes while searching for food. It dives 1500 feet and can chase down a squid or small fish if it chooses. One weddell seal was timed during its dive, and was below the surface for 43 minutes.

Seals are capable of changing their heartbeats during a dive. Normally their rate is 150 beats per minute on the surface. During a dive they reduce it to a mere ten a minute. They live off the oxygen already in their bodies. The seal's system doesn't worry about it. Some species of seal can even sleep under water.

The weddell seal is destined to a jolly life. They weigh a plump 60 pounds at birth. And after only two weeks of nursing on mother's butterfat milk, junior quickly doubles his weight. However, by the time she has finished feeding her pups, the mother seal loses a total of 300 pounds and is thoroughly worn out.

A mother weddell seal becomes completely disoriented at the sight of danger. If an intruder threatens her, she reacts by killing her young pups. However, the mother does care and will remain with her pup for days after it has died.

These seals love ice so intensely they choose to live under it during the winter. They make holes for air with their teeth. In later life they often have badly worn teeth.

All of these seals lead active lives. But in case it's necessary, they also have a retirement plan which isn't too bad. When weddell seals become elderly, injured, or sick, they climb to high country. They have been found 35 miles from shores and 3,000 feet above sea level. This keeps them out of the competitive world but still gives plenty of cold snow and ice. There they either recover or live out the rest of their lives surrounded by cold beauty.

When we travel to the farthest tips of the world, the evidence of God's work is startling—the beautiful sunsets, the pure air, and the fascinating life of little-known creatures. Far from being barren ice land, it is rich with the glory of God.

"He quiets the raging oceans and all the world's clamor. In the farthest corners of the earth the glorious acts of God shall startle everyone. The dawn and sunset shout for joy" (Ps. 65:7, 8, TLB).

1. How long can a weddell seal stay under water?
2. Where do they go to "retire" or "heal"?
3. Name some beautiful places that you have seen which God has made.

Thank you, God, for a beautiful world.

thirty-five

City Under the Sea

What will the ocean be like a hundred years from now? Will there be domed cities like giant shopping malls? Maybe there will be regular bus service running from land down to 2,000 feet beneath the sea.

Before we laugh at this, look back 100 years. There were no airplanes or automobiles. If you had said that man could land on the moon, most people would have considered you goofy.

In the next 100 years changes may come much faster. Your grandchildren may take vacations in a city called Atlantis and watch the squids swim by.

Would you be surprised to learn that some scientists already live under the sea? Men have spent weeks in aqua-labs. All of their activities and studies take place inside a submerged apartment.

Not only will people work under the sea but so will mobots. Mobots are underwater robots. They can be controlled to help man in his work.

When the time comes to visit the sea, don't be afraid to go. Underwater travel may be safer than on the surface. For one thing, storms will probably have no effect on the sea-buses.

Tomorrow's city will be built on the dreams of the famous oceanographer, Jacques-Yves Cousteau. He has already built a village on the bottom of the Red Sea, and people have lived in it. As Cousteau has said, "One day soon, men will walk on the ocean floor as they do down the street."

The hope is that men will not be restricted to buildings, submarines, and buses. Some scientists believe men will wear simple headgear with mechanical gills and take pills to prevent them from getting sick from the depths.

Part of the reason why cities do not already exist is that we do not put the same importance on the sea as we have on space. However, it now looks like man will soon live in the sea.

No dream is impossible, especially if God wants it to happen. He has given us amazing abilities, fascinating materials, and tremendous minds. If we dedicate all of these to Him, He may be waiting to use us in ways we never imagined.

Many of the world's great scientists have been Christians. Possibly God plans to use your mind for some of the great wonders under the sea.

"I know the greatness of the Lord—that he is greater far than any other god. He does whatever pleases him throughout all of heaven and earth, and in the deepest seas" (Ps. 135:6, TLB).

1. What is a mobot?
2. Make up a name for a city under the sea.
3. What amazing thing would you like to see God do?

Thank you for a fascinating world, heavenly Father.

thirty-six

Swimming Snakes

Have you ever seen a snake do a head stand? Can you imagine one with its tail sticking straight up? Some underwater snakes do exactly this. They are hunting fish eggs for dinner. The snake buries its head in the sand and leaves its tail high in the water.

Some can swim backwards almost as fast as they swim forward.

Not only does this snake gobble down fish eggs, but it also swallows small stones. The stones don't hurt him.

You don't need to worry about the snake's safety. It's true that it can't see or defend itself in this strange position, but the fish merely pass by. This type of snake is so poisonous everything stays away from it.

Despite its dangerous bite, the sea snake does have a few enemies. The sea eagle not only isn't afraid of this snake, but it also hunts him for supper. This eagle must really have a strong stomach in order to eat so much poison.

The sea snake's other enemy is man. Man often invades the watery world of this creature and hunts it. Sometimes, however, he loses this battle and becomes the victim. Most of the time, though, people are successful. Asians often capture sea snakes for food. Some people love good roasted snake. They also earn money by selling the colorful skin.

Most sea snakes spend their entire lives in the water, but there are a few exceptions. A snake near Japan comes ashore to reproduce. While there, it will roam around the villages and steal fish left out to dry. These snakes must be a scary sight since they sometimes are four-and-a-half feet in length.

Sea snakes are usually small, but a few are enormous. One variety reaches 25 feet. Not only are they long, but they are also fast. Some can swim backwards almost as fast as they swim forward. Their rapid tail gives them excellent speed.

Generally, water is safe for swimming. Very few people are ever bitten by sea snakes. In most cases the snake is interested in getting away from people. Most areas do not have poisonous sea snakes.

If you see a snake, the safest thing is to stay away from it until you know what kind it is. Your parents might be able to help you identify it.

Most snake bites do not kill but only make the person sick. The Bible tells us that getting drunk and being bitten by a snake are much alike. Both can make you dizzy and change your behavior. You may not be able to think straight and you might say stupid things. You also could become terribly sick to your stomach.

We do not want to be bitten by snakes. Neither does it make any sense to get drunk.

"Don't let the sparkle and smooth taste of strong wine de-

ceive you. For in the end it bites like a poisonous serpent; it stings like an adder. You will see hallucinations and have delirium tremens, and you will say foolish, silly things that would embarrass you no end when sober" (Prov. 23:31-33, TLB).

1. How do snakes hunt fish eggs?
2. What hunts sea snakes?
3. What does your family think about alcoholic beverages?

Keep our minds clear, Holy Spirit.

thirty-seven

The Leatherback

During the days of ancient Rome the person who caught a sea turtle was well off. He could use practically every part of the reptile.

If there were any hair problems in the family, turtle blood was put on his head. They thought it could restore hair and wipe out dandruff. For those who had healthy hair, turtle gall could still be helpful for dying the hair yellow.

Turtle blood made an excellent whitener for teeth or cure for a toothache. Even earaches could be cleared up with a dose of it.

The largest sea turtle is the leatherback. It isn't unusual for them to reach eight feet and weigh 1,500 pounds. If they could be trained they are large enough to pull an 18-foot sailboat.

Despite its huge size the leatherback has a special diet. It feeds mostly on jellyfish and the Portuguese man-of-war. These morsels are 95 percent water. The leatherback has to eat carloads of them to keep his large factory operating.

There is no other reptile which roams such a large part of the world. They roam the coasts of Norway north of the Arctic Circle as well as the southern shores of New Zealand. The leatherback may visit the shores of Japan or make a casual call on Chile.

Normally they live to be older than humans and reproduce freely. Possibly four times each year the female comes ashore to lay eggs. She deposits 90-150 eggs per trip.

It's doubtful these large reptiles merely wander the seas aimlessly. They probably follow patterns and are able to find mates. So far their system has escaped the understanding of man. To learn their swimming patterns might prove to be of considerable value to humanity.

So far the only person who fully understands the navigation

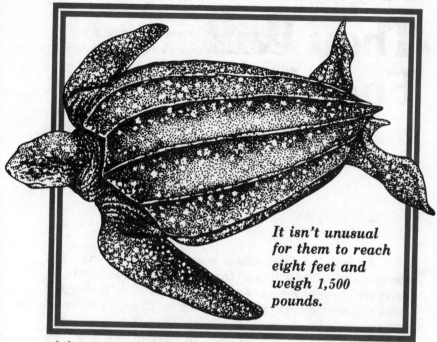

It isn't unusual for them to reach eight feet and weigh 1,500 pounds.

of the sea turtle is Jesus Christ. He created and controls them. Even in the dark, mysterious sea He knows where they are.

We never escape the watchful eye of Christ, either. We are not a mystery to Him. He knows when we fail and when we win. Jesus knows more about us than we know about ourselves. That's great! This makes it easier for Him to help us.

"Christ himself is the Creator who made everything in heaven and earth, the things we can see and the things we can't; the spirit world with its kingdoms, its rulers and authorities; all were made by Christ for his own use and glory. He was before all else began and it is his power that holds everything together" (Col. 1:16, 17, TLB).

1. What do leatherbacks eat?
2. How many eggs does the female lay?
3. Where can you go to hide from Jesus Christ?

We thank you, our Creator, for holding us together.

thirty-eight

They Will Fool You

There is little to worry about when you go swimming. Most shores are safe. You will swim the rest of your life and probably never see anything more dangerous than a jellyfish. However, if you travel around the world, always find out about the water before you jump in.

If you swim in the Indian Ocean, you need to know about the zebra fish. Its large black and white stripes will make you want to go toward it. They have 18 spines sticking out all over their body. The problem is that these spines are deadly poisonous. Just a touch and you could be terribly ill or even paralyzed. Most people would recover, but not everyone.

The lionfish must be one of the loveliest sea creatures in the world. It has bright reddish colors and looks too fluffy to hurt anyone. Despite its beauty, a mere touch and a swimmer would be finished.

Not every deadly fish is colorful and cute. The stonefish is as ugly as mud. Its name describes it well. This little killer looks just like any rock you would find on the bottom of a lake. Unsuspecting walkers are likely to step on this creature in the Pacific Ocean.

Toadfish are gruesome looking. If you see it you will automatically keep your distance. Its four poisonous spines will not kill you, but they are terribly painful.

These are rare fish and not likely to be found anywhere near where we swim. However, it's always important to find out about what lives in the water where we intend to play or fish.

Fish will fool us, but so will people if we aren't careful. There are many religious groups that look like fun to join. They sound good but that doesn't make them godly. Often these groups are really cults. They look harmless.

We need to be careful of groups that do not put Jesus Christ first. We need to stay clear of people who insist we give complete obedience to them.

People are fooled because the group looks good. Later they may be terribly sorry they didn't follow Christ instead.

"Jesus told them, 'Don't let anyone fool you. For many will come claiming to be the Messiah, and will lead many astray' " *(Matt. 24:4, 5, TLB).*

1. Where is a zebra fish's poison?
2. What should a person do before swimming in a new place?
3. What is one way to know if a group is really Christian?

Help us, Lord, to keep our faith in you alone.

thirty-nine

Sunken Ships

The seas are filled with tremendous wealth. Much of its treasure comes from natural riches such as fish, kelp, and oil. However, there are also rare treasures from ancient sunken ships. Some of these ships have been found, and amazing amounts of gold, silver, mercury, and jewels have been discovered.

One of the most famous finds was from the ancient Spanish ship *San José*. The vessel sank near Florida in 1733. Over half a million dollars in gold and silver have been recovered.

The hunt for sunken treasure sounds exciting, but usually it begins in a dusty library. Explorers must first study the records of ships, their destiny and their cargo. The adventurer needs to know for sure that there are riches worth the risk.

Sometimes the sunken treasure provides great riches; however, more often than not the searchers are fortunate if they don't lose money.

But not everyone who looks for treasure ends up penniless. One man has raised millions of dollars to the surface, including several coins worth $12,000 apiece. A necklace found off a Florida shore sold for $50,000.

Few attempts at recovering old ships are as remarkable as the raising of the *Vasa*. This vessel sank over 300 years ago and had been forgotten until someone ran across the name. The Swedish government was told about it, and they raised the entire ship. Today it rests in a museum with most of its original possessions still on it.

A couple of teenage boys unexpectedly found some rare treasure while in the Pacific Ocean. The swimmers discovered a large supply of coins and a small bronze cannon. Their finds dated back to 1702.

Recently a sunken ship was found with an unusual treasure on it. The *Tolosa* sank off the shore of Santo Domingo in 1724. Among the many treasures found was over 3 million dollars worth of quicksilver or mercury.

It must be tremendously exciting to find sunken treasure. Most of us are not going to find gold off the Florida Keys. However, we could find a treasure worth far more. Many things in life are worth more than gold. Mothers, fathers, friends are each a great treasure.

The Bible speaks of real wealth. It says if we have to choose between riches and a good name, always select a good name.

It's more important that people know you are honest and dependable. If people can trust you, you are already rich.

"If you must choose, take a good name rather than great riches; for to be held in loving esteem is better than silver and gold" (Prov. 22:1, TLB).

1. Who raised the *Vasa*?
2. What was on the *Tolosa*?
3. How can you have a good name?

Help us to see what is really valuable, Lord.

forty

Private Detectives

Have you ever seen a small head covered with bushy whiskers bob out of the water? If you have, you know how much fun it is to watch seals. We spotted them all over the Puget Sound in Washington State. Seals are so quick and clever that they hunt salmon with little difficulty.

As man has gotten to know the seal, we have learned to enjoy its many abilities. They dive like submarines and are lightning fast. Seals can be taught a number of jobs besides playing horns in the circus.

The Navy has so much faith in the seal's intelligence that they are using them for difficult tasks. Sea lions are now being used as underwater detectives. Their skills have saved millions of dollars.

Many missiles are fired over the ocean and then fall into the deep waters. The Navy can practice with these weapons again if they can get them back. This is where the crafty sea lion detective comes in.

A large clamp is placed on the seal's nose and it dives for the ocean floor. In a few minutes the seal hunts down the lost object and bumps his nose against it. The clamp locks onto the weapon. Navy sailors have already tied a heavy cord to the clamp and now have little trouble recovering their treasure.

When the sea lion returns to the ship, it is hugged and fed plenty of good fish. The private detective has brought back its treasure.

Sea lions aren't the greatest brains in nature but neither are they dumb. What really makes them important is that they are teachable. When they are told what to do, they can respond and usually do it correctly.

You and I have far more ability to learn than a sea lion. We may not be able to swim as well but we certainly think better.

Because humans are so intelligent and trainable, God decided to teach us through a book. The Bible is packed with good, wise guidance for our lives. It may not make us swim any better, but it certainly will save us from a great many troubles. The really smart young person lets the Bible speak to him.

"Follow my advice, my son; always keep it in mind and stick to it" (Prov. 7:1, TLB).

1. How does the Navy use sea lions?
2. How does the clamp work?
3. Name something the Bible has taught you.

Keep our minds open and teachable, Holy Spirit.

Seals can be taught a number of jobs besides playing horns in the circus.

forty-one

How Many Arms?

Do you want to think about something spooky? There are millions and millions of arms moving around the ocean. Some of the arms are small like the ones on starfish. Others are gigantic like the ones which cover the huge squid and octopuses.

How long are squid arms? No one knows for sure. Most squids live deep in the sea and have never been seen by man. The largest squid ever found was in 1888. Each of its arms measured about 20 feet long.

It isn't just the length of the arms that is amazing; it is also the number. An octopus has eight creepy arms. His relative, the squid, carries ten.

Each arm is covered with suction cups. Every cup grabs with enough force to leave a terrible red mark on your body.

How many of these multiple-armed creatures are swimming around in the ocean? No one can say. We do know that sometimes sailors have been fooled in measuring the ocean. They thought they had found the bottom only to learn that it was a "false bottom" made up of thousands of squid.

Since the giant squid live deep in the ocean, there is little for us to fear. However, once in a great while one of these monsters has come to the top.

On a few occasions an octopus or a squid has wrapped its arms, called tentacles, around a small boat. Usually quick-thinking sailors grab hatchets and begin to cut off the arms. My fisherman friend did this after bringing up a large octopus on his line.

These attacks are rare in history; and when it has happened,

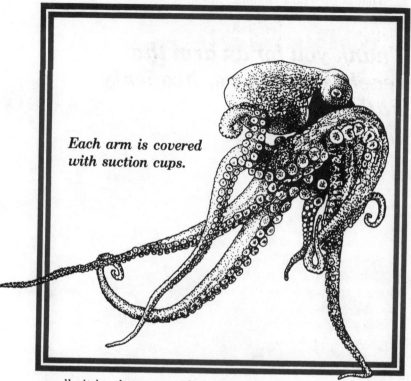

Each arm is covered with suction cups.

usually it has been a squid. Octopuses are generally shy and often will try to get away.

Normally there isn't anything to worry about. People swim in the sea and do it safely. There millions or billions of arms won't bother you.

Arms do not have to be bad. Do you remember resting on your parents' arms and thinking about how good it felt? You could depend on them and their love.

When God speaks of His arm, He is talking about the same feeling. In times of stress and in times of happiness we can relax in the arms of God. Even though we cannot see Him, God wants us to lean back upon Him.

"My righteousness is near; my salvation is gone forth, and mine arms shall judge the people; the isles shall wait upon me, and on mine arm shall they trust" (Isa. 51:5, KJV).

1. Which creature has ten arms?

2. What is the "false bottom" in the ocean?
3. When does it feel good to lean back upon God's arms?

Thank you for an arm that reaches out to us, heavenly Father.

forty-two

The Secret of the Submarine

How do submarines work? When they dive under the water, what stops them from sinking to the bottom? How can they come up whenever they want to?

Many people in history have tried to develop a submarine, but not until 1776 did David Bushnell put one to use. His vessel looked like a large ball. It was made of wood and could stay 12 feet under the surface. Called the *Turtle*, this vessel was moved by a hand-cranked propeller.

The *Turtle* attacked a British ship by trying to attach an explosive to the ship's bottom. Bushnell was surprised to find the bottom of the ship covered with copper. The *Turtle* was spotted by the crew and barely escaped.

There was no hope of putting submarines in the sea as long as they had to be moved by a hand-driven propeller. Fuel was also a big problem for submarines. How could they carry enough diesel or gas to travel long distances? Fortunately, this problem has been solved for modern submarines: nuclear subs can circle the earth twice on a lump of uranium about the size of one baseball.

Submarines have come a long way since the *Turtle*. Modern subs can go around the world completely under water.

How did inventors solve the submarine's big problem of going up and down? Submarines have a number of ballast tanks built into the bottom or hull. When these tanks hold air the submarine stays on top. If it wants to dive, water is taken into the ballast tanks. This adds weight and causes the sub to go down. When the sub is to surface, the water is merely pumped out of the tanks.

People have learned to control the tanks. If they want to dive 20 feet or 40 feet, they take on just the right amount of water. The crew must carefully check the water/air balance to keep the submarine under control. Otherwise it will sink like a rock or bounce up onto the surface.

Life has its ups and downs like a submarine. When something goes wrong, we often "sink" and feel terrible. Maybe we weren't chosen for something or maybe we failed a test. It's no fun to feel down.

"You have let me sink down deep in desperate problems. But you will bring me back to life again, up from the depths of the earth" (Ps. 71:20, TLB).

1. Describe Bushnell's submarine.
2. How does a ballast tank work?
3. What gets you "down"? What brings you "up"?

Thanks, Lord, for giving our lives ballast tanks.

forty-three

Save the Sea Cows!

The manatee is a bulky, friendly creature that likes to munch on soft vegetation. On a good day a manatee can eat 100 pounds of seaweed. Today there are laws to protect this sea cow, but that wasn't always true. Not long ago manatees were almost hunted out of existence.

Manatees are mammals. They are warm-blooded, have backbones, and give milk to their young. However, despite their size of over 12 feet, they are practically helpless on land. The manatee lives well under water but has to come up every 10 or 15 minutes to breathe.

In some ways the sea cows seem almost human. They lead very calm lives and especially enjoy getting together. Once in a while you can see them kiss or hold flippers as they swim. Both the mother and father manatee make good parents. The ones that live in captivity are easy to care for and appear happy.

When ancient sailors first saw the manatee, they thought the cows were half-human mermaids. The seamen must have been away from land a long time for their eyes to fool them that much.

The manatee used to have a relative that lived in the cold Bering Sea. They were called stellers. This huge cousin weighed over three tons and was 30 feet in length. Whalers hunted the steller without caring how many they took.

Today there are no stellers left. They have not been seen for 150 years. If laws had not been passed to protect the manatee, they could also have become extinct.

Animals are not as valuable as people, but they certainly are important. Nature would lose its balance if we killed off too many. Animals of both the land and sea help make our life more interesting.

God wants us to use His world and to preserve it. If we over-hunt without caring what happens, we could cause many creatures to become extinct.

"Your future is as solid as God's mountains. Your decisions are as full of wisdom as the oceans are with water. You are concerned for men and animals alike" (Ps. 36:6, TLB).

1. What did the ancient sailors think a manatee was?
2. What happened to the steller?
3. How can we help protect animals from being over-hunted?

If we are to keep animals, we must be wise. Lord, give us wisdom.

In some ways the sea cows seem almost human. They lead very calm lives and especially enjoy getting together.

forty-four

Swordfish Attack

Think twice before you go fishing for the powerful swordfish. They are hard to catch and once hooked may decide to attack the fisherman. However, if you do manage to bring one in, it will make excellent eating.

Swordfish like to roam around at great depths, and this makes them difficult to find. Some of their favorite foods are jellyfish and squid. Often the squid comes close to the surface, and that's the best time to look for swordfish.

The sword attached to the nose of this fish is not a toy. It is strong enough to pierce hard surfaces and often has. Most of the time the swordfish uses its spear to slash through schools of fish.

When a swordfish is caught, it might charge the boat. It must be a frightening sight—a 400-, 600-, maybe even 1,000-pound fish racing through the water and heading directly for the vessel. With back fin slicing through the surface, the swordfish can drive a dreadful hole in the boat's side.

Not only might the fish attack, but its friends could join in. Sometimes six swordfish have charged a boat at one time.

Don't be surprised if you cut your line after a swordfish attacks. They have hit boats a dozen times before the fishermen have cut them loose, but it is usually the men who give up, not the fish.

Despite their ability to puncture a vessel, they are still hunted. Hundreds of swordfish are caught off the Florida coast alone.

One of the strangest attacks happened when no one was fishing. The small submarine, *Alvin*, was near the Carolina coast

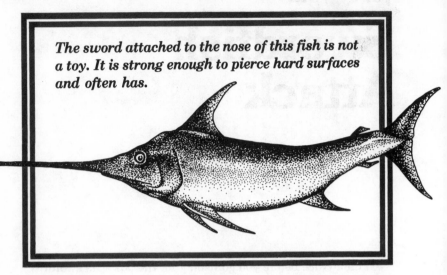

The sword attached to the nose of this fish is not a toy. It is strong enough to pierce hard surfaces and often has.

when, without warning, a swordfish charged. Evidently frightened by the sub's lights, the fish used his sword to pierce the *Alvin's* seam. The submarine surfaced immediately, glad that the damage was no more serious than a puncture hole.

Fortunately not many people carry swords. However, sometimes people are just as dangerous as any swordfish. Some will enjoy spreading lies about others. The Bible tells us it's just like piercing them with a sword. Sometimes it does as much damage.

We should be careful how we talk about others. It's easy to hurt people with words, and not nearly as easy to heal the injury.

If someone lied about us, we would feel unhappy. God wants us to be sure not to stab others with a sharp sword called lies.

"Telling lies about someone is as harmful as hitting him with an axe, or wounding him with a sword, or shooting him with a sharp arrow" (Prov. 25:18, TLB).

1. What do swordfish eat?
2. What happened to the *Alvin*?
3. Has someone ever lied about you? Without mentioning their name, tell how you felt.

Help us guard what we say, Holy Spirit.

forty-five

Seashells Are Noisy

Have you ever picked up a seashell and held it to your ear? Do you wonder what causes that sound? Is it the echo of the sea?

Naturally there are some shells you can't pick up. The giant clam can grow to four feet in length and weigh a robust 500 pounds.

If you live near Australia, there are some shells you won't dare lift. The Toxoglossa is blamed for killing 20 people with its poisonous bite and making many others sick.

In old Africa you would not have thrown away many shells. Some countries use them as a form of money. A shipment of shells can purchase food or a good elephant tusk.

You shouldn't count on seeing every type of seashell. To do that you would have to climb 15,000 feet up into the mountains and dive 25,000 feet into the sea. Even then, there are so many thousands of varieties you couldn't hope to see them all.

When you pick up one colorful shell and hold it to your ear, you can hear an amazing sound, like ocean waves. What causes it?

A well-formed seashell is so finely made it can pick up any movement in the air. The little sounds bounce around inside like the echo of the seashores. Sometimes you will be able to hear sounds in the shell that are not loud enough otherwise for your ears.

Nature is filled with fascinating noises. Noise isn't always bad; in its right place noise can be a gift. Used correctly, noise can be used to worship God.

Have you ever been so happy you felt you just had to make

109

noise? Have you ever been so filled with joy that you wanted to shout "Thank God!"? Maybe someday you should go ahead and do it. In your living room, in the basement, or in your backyard, look up and shout, "Thank God!" It's one of the best ways we can use noise.

"Shout with joy before the Lord, O earth! Obey him gladly; come before him, singing with joy" (Ps. 100:1, 2, TLB).

1. How big do clams get?
2. Where are shells found?
3. When was the last time you felt like shouting to God?

There are joyful noises. We use them to praise you, God.

forty-six

The Beaches Come Alive

Every spring an amazing thing happens along the beaches of Southern California. Thousands of small fish called grunions come in with the tide to lay their eggs.

The mother grunion wiggles her tail into the soft sand and sticks her head almost straight up. She deposits thousands of eggs just a couple of inches deep in the sand.

When the female catches the tide out, the eggs are left on their own. The eggs lay quietly in the moist, warm sand and wait for the right moment to hatch.

Two weeks later their time comes. A tide washes ashore and uncovers the eggs. When the eggs pop to the top they begin to hatch. Thousands of newborn grunions begin twisting and turning on the sand. When the tide begins to go out to sea, the baby grunions take a free ride to the open ocean.

Grunions have become a big attraction in California. Many spectators come to watch the unusual event. Some bring buckets and catch what they can with their bare hands.

The grunion is of the silverside family and is supposed to make excellent eating.

We don't know if we will see them, but someday God will raise dead bodies from their graves, similar to the grunions coming out of the sand. The bodies will be taken to heaven and re-united with the real person. When that happens, God will have begun the great resurrection of believers in Jesus Christ.

"For the Lord himself will come down from heaven with a mighty shout and with the soul-stirring cry of the archangel and

the great trumpet-call of God. And the believers who are dead will be the first to rise to meet the Lord" (1 Thess. 4:16, TLB).

1. How deep are grunion eggs placed in the sand?
2. How do baby grunions get to the sea?
3. What noises will be sounded when Jesus returns?

Even though we die, Lord, we look forward to eternal life with you.

forty-seven

Are Eels Really Electric?

When I was a child I was afraid to touch an eel. One day I caught one on a line and no one else would grab it, either. We were all afraid we would be shocked or even electrocuted. We weren't sure that eels carried electricity, but none of us wanted to find out the hard way.

Now we know, however. There is both good news and bad news. The bad news is that there really are electric eels that can shock us. The good news is that most of these powerful eels live in South America around the Amazon River.

There the electric eel can grow to seven feet long. Their gills are so small they have to come to the surface every fifteen minutes to breathe.

There are many fish which carry an electric shock. However, most of the 250 species give off no more than 50 volts and aren't dangerous to people. However, the electric eel carries 600 volts. Fortunately, it does not shock with its full strength.

Electric eels have other strange features also. For one thing they have detachable tails. If something grabs onto the eel's tail, it merely drops its tail and takes off, leaving the attacker bewildered.

Another odd thing about the eel is the location of most of the eel organs. Its important body parts are up around its head and neck. This is why eels are often round at the head and slender in the body.

The electric eel doesn't have many enemies. Eels shock fish easily and turn them into a meal, so most fish try to stay away from them.

If something grabs onto the eel's tail, it merely drops its tail and takes off, leaving the attacker bewildered.

An eel's electricity is just like the kind you have at home. If you could connect an eel to your home, it would turn your lights on. However, after giving its first big shock it needs to rest its batteries before it can make more electricity.

Wouldn't it be neat if we could slip an electric eel into our flashlight? Then we wouldn't need any batteries. Or how about strapping a big eel inside our car to make it run?

Here is a better idea. Whenever we are facing difficult circumstances or need power to do the right thing, why don't we ask God to help us use His power inside us? God is very strong and wise. And He especially likes to help us.

"God is our refuge and strength, a tested help in times of trouble" (Ps. 46:1, TLB).

1. Where do the most powerful electric eels live?
2. What is strange about an electric eel's tail?
3. When would you like to have God help you?

Thanks for your great power, dear God.

forty-eight

Strange Stories

Do you ever wonder how some stories ever get started? The ancient Greeks called the electric ray a narke. Our word narcotics comes from this word. The Greeks called it a narke because they believed this ray could cast a spell on people. They thought fishermen should be especially careful of its magic power.

The Greeks also believed a person could remove hair by collecting electric ray brains. If a woman merely had this fish nearby, it was supposed to make childbirth easier.

Some island people have believed that sharks are actually gods and have worshipped them. Temples and altars have been built to keep these sharks happy.

In Samoa many people believed sharks punished thieves. If someone stole something, they believed that the next time he went to sea he would be eaten.

The John Dory is a fish that has an odd story. Some of these fish live in the Mediterranean Sea. They are unique because they have a large black spot on each side. According to legends this was a mark left by the Apostle Peter when he picked up the fish and found money in its mouth.

One group of Indians believed that the earth began on the back of a turtle. They taught that a gigantic turtle came up out of the sea and plants began to form and grow on its shell. For years they told their children that the world was riding on a turtle.

Ancient mythology teaches that Venus came from the sea. When she was born she was already an adult and immediately set sail for dry ground on a scallop shell.

It's fun to listen to stories whether they are true or made up. Both children and adults enjoy listening, learning, and reading.

We should know when a story is true and when it is only a made-up one.

One of the best parts of life is hearing the true story about God and His love for us. It's fascinating to hear about His son, Jesus Chrsit, and all that He has done. It's even more interesting to know that the life, death, and resurrection of Jesus Christ is totally true.

"And this is the way to have eternal life—by knowing you, the only true God, and Jesus Christ, the one you sent to earth" (John 17:3, TLB).

1. How did the Greeks try to remove hair?
2. One group of Indians believe that the earth began where?
3. How much of the story of Jesus Christ is true?

We thank you, Lord, that the true story about Jesus has been given in the Bible.

forty-nine

The Singing Penguins

Do you have trouble telling one penguin from another? Evidently the emperor penguins have the same problem. So, in order to solve this problem, they sing. Singing helps them to find and recognize each other.

These penguins apparently have real problems. They can't tell the girl penguins from the boy penguins. When they meet they politely bow to each other and then start to sing. The female has a gentle tone while the male sings loud and long.

It's difficult to imagine what they sing about, though. They live in the coldest place in the world. The temperature in the Antarctic often drops to 80 degrees below zero. Yet the cold doesn't seem to bother them at all. The emperor picks the dead of winter to lay eggs and hatch chickens.

When hundreds of emperor penguins come together into a huge choir, what a noise they make! All of them are singing and looking for a mate. The entire group together is called a turtle.

The mother lays her eggs in May, which is the cold fall in Antarctica. Instead of a warm, soft nest, the egg is placed on the cold, open ice.

When the father sees the egg he breaks into a solo. Mother pushes the egg over to the father. He sits on it and sings some more choruses.

How does all this happy singing affect the babies? It doesn't take long to find out. If you place your ear close to the egg shell, you can hear the unborn chick singing. It won't be long before it joins the enormous choir.

Emperor penguins aren't the greatest parents in nature. Many chicks become lost and die. The only way a chick can find its parents is to sing a few bars. It hopes to soon hear a familiar song and know its parents are near.

We aren't emperor penguins, but most of us enjoy singing. Songs are important in nature, but they are also important to people. We have many reasons to sing, but none better than to sing praises to God.

It doesn't take a great voice to sing to God. He wants to hear what we feel. When our hearts are filled with love and thanksgiving, singing comes easier.

"Sing to the Lord, for he has done wonderful things. Make known his praise around the world" (Isa. 12:5, TLB).

1. In connection with penguins, what is a turtle?
2. When do emperor chicks begin singing?
3. What is your favorite hymn?

We thank you, God, for giving us a reason to sing.

Puffed-Up Toads

If there are toads living near you, be thankful. This little relative of the frog is your friend. Every day it works hard to keep the insect population down.

Toads are such good insect eaters that some farmers have bought them and placed them near their crops. In South America they help protect the sugar-cane fields.

Most toads stay out of the water whenever they can, but they need to live near a pond. They lay their eggs in watery areas. If you have a couple of toads, you may soon have thousands. A female toad sometimes lays 20,000 eggs in one year. Toad eggs later open to become the long-tailed tadpoles we see so often.

The toad population is kept down by its many enemies. Birds, skunks, even dogs and other animals love a good toad snack. However, the greenish creature is not completely defenseless. Toads have small glands behind their eyes which shoot a sickening liquid. Not only will this make most attackers retreat, but in cases where the creatures are small, it can kill.

If everything works correctly, nature stays in good balance. Toads eat insects and skunks eat toads. Hopefully this stops the population of any creature from becoming too great. If either of these fails to do its job, parts of the world end up with too many insects or too many toads. God created them to feed off each other.

The male toad has a fascinating way to let the female toad know he's around. He sits by the side of a pond and croaks. His sound is different from any other creature.

At the same time the toad puffs up its throat to a huge size. When he does this, his throat sends out a pale light to make him a little easier to locate.

The male toad sits there filled with pride as he puffs his throat. In effect he is saying, "Look at me, girls. Have you ever seen such a good-looking toad?"

Maybe the Apostle Paul had toads in his backyard. Several times he told people not to get puffed up. He was talking to people who like to brag. Oftentimes we like to claim we are better than we really are. It's like puffing up and saying, "Look at me. I'm terrific."

There is nothing wrong with knowing you are a good ballplayer. You can thank God for that. Neither is there anything wrong with knowing you can read well. You can thank God for that, too.

The problem is, however, that we often like to brag and we forget to thank God. That's being puffed up. The well-balanced person knows he or she can do things and thanks God for those abilities.

"What are you so puffed up about? What do you have that God hasn't given you? And if all you have is from God, why act as though you are so great, and as though you have accomplished something on your own?" (1 Cor. 4:7, TLB).

1. How do toads defend themselves?
2. Where do toads lay eggs?
3. What does "puffed up" mean when people do it?

Praise God for all He has given us!

fifty-one

The Team Shark

It isn't always pleasant to think about, but most sea creatures live by eating other sea creatures. This is the way God made them. It's a perfectly normal part of nature.

One of the most interesting hunters in the ocean is a shark named the thresher. These sharks are harmless to man, but they eat great amounts of fish.

A thresher's tail is its outstanding feature. It is often as long as the rest of the shark's body. It gets its name from its unusually long tail and the way it uses it. When a thresher sees a school of fish, it surrounds them with its long tail. The fish become frightened and pull into a tight circle. This makes it easy for the shark to get a large dinner in one big gulp.

Man doesn't know much else about the thresher. Few of them have ever been caught, though once in a while one might get tangled in a fishing net. Possibly most of these sharks live far out to sea and at depths where man has seldom been.

Normally the thresher does well fishing alone. However, some fishermen believe it is also a team shark. Once in a while two of them will cooperate in herding fish together. When their prey are collected, both sharks share in the meal.

Maybe thresher sharks are much like people. There are times when we get along well alone. Often we are even better off by ourselves. However, there are some times when we need the help of others.

There are usually plenty of things to do in our rooms or playing in the backyard. However, it isn't good to be alone all the time. That extra person or team can be a great help when we need someone around.

That's why Christian friends are important. We need others

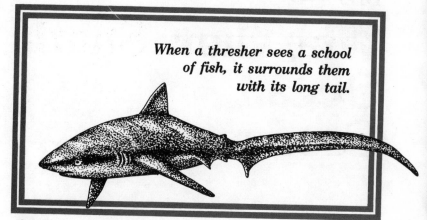

When a thresher sees a school of fish, it surrounds them with its long tail.

who can be a good influence on us. We also need to be a good influence on our friends.

Jesus understood that adults need other adults and children need children. Life goes so much better if we can gather a few kind, Christian friends around us.

"After these things the Lord appointed other seventy also, and sent them two and two before his face into every city and place, whither he himself would come" (Luke 10:1, KJV).

1. How does a thresher get its name?
2. How do two threshers work together?
3. Why do we need Christian friends?

Thanks, Lord Jesus, for friends we can count on.

fifty-two

Why the Ocean Groans

When God made the oceans they were beautiful places. They are still lovely, but if man isn't careful our seas will become polluted and ugly.

Some lakes and rivers that used to be plentiful with fish are now "dead seas." The government has had to prohibit fishing in a few areas because of too many harmful chemicals in the water.

A scientist was asked to test the water in a certain river. He collected the samples and left them. When he came back the water was gone; in an hour and a half the acids had eaten the bottom out of the bucket. This is unusual, but it shows how bad things can get.

Many things pollute our waters. Sewage, industrial run-off, and agriculture can all be harmful. One of the biggest problems is oil spills. In one year a gigantic oil spill in the English Channel resulted in the death of 25,000 seabirds. There was a large oil spill off the southern coast of California. Ten years later some varieties of marine life had not yet returned to the area.

It is estimated that 4,000 oil tankers are sailing the open seas. There are 3,000 drilling platforms around the United States.

In the past we thought our waters could handle anything. We have dumped waste, chemicals, and garbage into them. One ocean explorer says he has seen pollution all over the world.

Hopefully we are smart enough to turn this around. Many industries are changing their methods of dumping waste. Oil companies are taking added precautions. Some lakes and rivers that were "dead" now have fish again.

We have abused God's gift of water. We have made it ugly and unsafe. By being careful and considerate we still have time to correct our mistakes and keep water as a helpful resource.

Human beings do some highly intelligent things. We are also capable of destroying nature. God has left the choice up to us.

"For all creation is waiting patiently and hopefully for that future day when God will resurrect his children. For on that day thorns and thistles, sin, death, and decay—the things that overcame the world against its will at God's command—will all disappear, and the world around us will share in the glorious freedom from sin which God's children will enjoy" (Rom. 8:19-21, TLB).

1. What causes sea pollution?
2. How can we help stop it?
3. How else can we protect God's world?

Thank you for a beautiful world, heavenly Father. Help us to know how to protect it.